THE SOAP OPERA BOOK

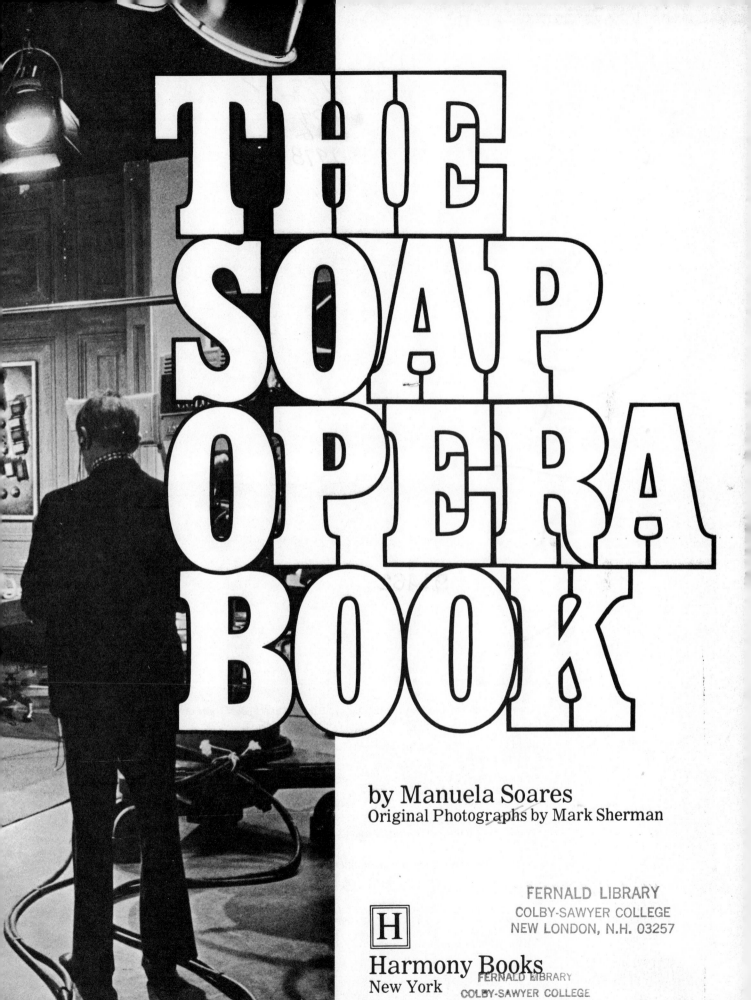

THE SOAP OPERA BOOK

by Manuela Soares
Original Photographs by Mark Sherman

Harmony Books
New York

Book Design by Jan V. White
Cover Design by Ken Sansone

Harmony Books
a division of Crown Publishers, Inc.
One Park Avenue, New York, New York 10016

Printed in the United States of America. Published simultaneously in
Canada by General Publishing Company Ltd.

Library of Congress Cataloging in Publication Data
Soares, Manuela.
    The soap opera book.

    1.   Soap operas—United States.   I.   Title.
PN1992.8.S4S6   791.45'5   77-17469
ISBN 0-517-533308
ISBN 0-517-533316 pbk.

Second Printing

CONTENTS

PREFACE

When I was approached about a book on soap operas, the idea immediately appealed to me. It's always been obvious that, with the exception of fan magazines and a few paperback books each year, the field of daytime serials has been sorely neglected. We soon found, however, that we could easily write ten books on such a broad and intricate topic as daytime serials. In *The Soap Opera Book,* we have tried to include topics that aren't generally discussed in the fan magazines. We wanted our book to explore as many aspects of the serials as possible - where they originate, how they're made, who watches them and why, and include as many original photographs as we could. At the same time, we wanted to find out how serials have changed over the years, and what were the differences, in story, sets, characters, and ideas, among all the current serial dramas. To accomplish this, we spoke not only to producers, directors, performers, writers, technicians, and set designers, but to the viewers themselves.

Looking back on soap opera history, we found that when anyone wrote about the serials, it was almost always in a negative sense. The critics have had a field day putting down serials for the past fifty years. Lately, however, this attitude has begun to change. In putting together the book, we wanted to look at both sides—what makes a good soap and a bad one. Every viewer knows that some serials are better than others, and we've explored the reasons why. In doing so, we looked at what goes into making serials, and how the people involved feel about them.

Even after several years of working in the soap opera field, I was surprised to find that almost everyone, from producers to viewers, had a different idea about what makes a good serial. I'd like to point out that the opinions expressed in the book are neither right nor wrong - they are simply the opinions of people who have been producing, directing, writing, and watching serials for many years. Sometimes you may agree, and sometimes you may not.

One of the difficulties in doing this book was that the serials move so quickly. The first critic (certainly not the last) who said serials move slowly, couldn't have ever watched them. Not only do actors and actresses playing a role change with some frequency, but sometimes the characters themselves change at an even quicker pace. As writers are replaced, even storyline emphasis can change.

The Soap Opera Book is as up-to-date as we can make it. But, I know in my heart, and from past experience, that by the time this book reaches you, John and Pat may be back together; Nancy may have adopted Timmy; Pat and Tony may have wed; and I shudder to think of how many characters may have been murdered or killed in accidents! Events like these may quickly outdate a cast list, but they don't affect who watches the serials, how they're made, where they started, and where they're going. And that, essentially, is what *The Soap Opera Book* is all about. So sit back, relax, and read about everything you always wanted to know about soap operas. The times that made you once afraid to ask are changing; soap operas have come into their own.

MGS

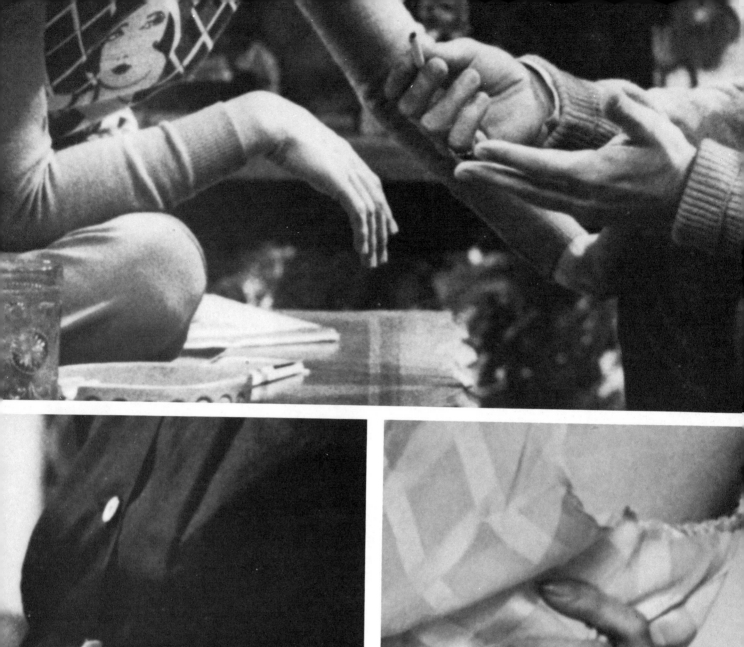

THE SOAP OPERA CRAZE

The big news in mass media entertainment this year is *story*. Everyone, from network executive to bearded offbeat journalist, is trying to sell you one: a passionate paperback romance; a scandalous biography of your favorite politician; an adventure tale pre-plotted by terrorists. Story is what's big because it's what people can become *involved in*. Most involving—and on top of the popular culture—is the story that never ends: the serialized drama. This is called a "series" if it's on at night and sponsored by Mobil Oil, or a "soap opera" if it's on in the afternoon and sponsored by Procter & Gamble.

It is safe to say that of all the story forms, none is more involving than the soap opera. Superfans don't answer their phones between the hours of 11:30 a.m. and 4:30 p.m. Even a casual fan will literally risk her life to see an important episode. One psychologist confessed that she got into an automobile accident in an effort to get home and find out if a soap character was going to have an abortion!

Everybody's involved. Soaps have been around for more than forty years of, course, but suddenly they are an in thing. They dominate daytime television and, in some cities, you can see them at night too. There are (at this writing) fourteen of them, from the trendy *The Young and the Restless* to the traditional *As the World Turns*. The newest soap, *Lovers and Friends*, came in with the new year. Even night-time TV is beginning to catch on to the remarkable appeal of soap opera stories and format. Spoofy *Mary Hartman, Mary Hartman* was the biggest bedtime story of 1976; it shares with the soaps, among other things, the chief virtue of being on without fail Monday through Friday. Other big night-time events include soap-like shows like *Rich Man, Poor Man; Upstairs/Downstairs;* and *Executive Suite*. When viewers say that they wish these shows were on every night (and that the story moved faster), they are really wishing that these shows were more like *Search for Tomorrow*. All of a sudden, Americans have discovered the fun of being involved in the soaps.

As a result, soaps are chic in all social circles. They are pop culture and as such openly celebrated. Whereas actors once regarded soaps as a way to keep food on the table until they could achieve stage or screen success, soaps now impart their own stardom. Soap personalities are accorded every symbol of celebrity status. They are besieged by fans, as Agnes Nixon, the creator of *All My Children* learned when she was mobbed on a college campus. They are gossiped about; there are now nineteen newsstand publications devoted to daytime TV and its personalities. They are interviewed in the media by such people as Barbara Walters, Mike Douglas, and Tom Snyder. They are feted: Manhattan Borough President proclaimed one week in April, 1976, "*The Edge of Night* and Daytime Serial Week." And soap personalities are welcomed by almost everyone, including the families of candidates for President. One campaigner for Jimmy Carter was actress Ruth Warrick of *All My*

Children. She appeared at least once with another Carter campaigner who is an ardent fan of the show: Carter's mother, Lillian. Acceptance like this indicates just how successful soap opera has become.

How many people actually watch soaps is not known for certain. Estimates begin at twenty million and go as high as seventy million. While the latter figure might be high, it isn't outrageously so. People of all shapes, sizes, ages, races, etc., are joining the ranks. The daytime serial is no longer just a white working-class housewife's entertainment. The stereotype of the woman with a baby in one hand, her sewing in the other, a loaf of bread burning in the oven, and a soap opera in front of her nose is out. Anyone might be a soap fan. There's a businessman in Massachusetts, for example, who schedules his lunch hour so that he can take in his favorite soap. There's the secretary in New York who keeps a mini-portable in her desk drawer so that she can catch one or two soaps during the day. And there's Supreme Court Justice Thurgood Marshall, former Governor John Connally, writer Dan Wakefield, entertainers Sammy Davis, Jr. and Carol Burnett, pianist Van Cliburn, and many other celebrities who are avowed soap fans. No, there's no "typical" fan today, and if there ever was one, she went out with the icebox.

Of course, the people with the greatest opportunity to watch are those who are not employed full time outside the home—a group that includes many homemakers. And many housebound women do in fact watch soaps. According to the Nielsen ratings, women in the 18-40 age group comprise an estimated 62% of the soap opera audience, and women over 40 are another large audience segment. What's more, women in the 18-40 age group buy 75% of the products advertised. That explains why soap, related cleaning products, and cosmetics dominate the commercials—why viewers will seldom, if ever, see tires gripping the road or football players plugging a "manlier scent" before, during or after a soap opera. From the sponsor's viewpoint, the soaps are women's shows and likely to remain so.

Millions of men, however, would disagree. It has been estimated that 30% of the audience of *All My Children* is male and over 18. *Ryan's Hope* is another soap with a considerable following among men; a recent Nielsen survey indicated a figure of nearly 20%. These percentages might not seem astronomical, but they translate into several million men who watch soaps regularly (and suggest that many more might do so if they could).

There is among men in particular a new attitude. In the past, men (as well as some women) were inclined to put soaps down, in many cases without having ever seen one. That's changing. A woman from California reports: "Back in the days when I was tied to the house with young children....my husband made fun of the soaps I watched. No more! Not long ago, he found himself completely lost in a detailed discussion of the soaps, their fine actors, their social contribution, and their handling of delicate subjects....This discussion was in a group of well-educated, culturally oriented people...." Today, soap watchers include "culturally-oriented" men, as well as women: professors, factory workers, truck drivers, and commercial artists. At one New York City police precinct house, the now defunct *Somerset* was a daily favorite. That would have been astonishing in the 1950s; now it is almost commonplace.

The Nielsen ratings indicate that overall most soap opera viewers are women, with men and (another consumer category) young people making up a small and growing minority. That is gospel to networks and sponsors, and it is probably not far from truth. Still, one wonders if the daytime ratings give an accurate picture of audience size and makeup. The Nielsen Television Index measures *household* viewers. That is fine for night-time television because people are at home. But what about daytime? The ratings do not include television sets in offices, hotels, warehouses, shops, or television lounges where soaps aren't simply a pastime— they're a rage. Nor do the ratings reflect the uses of the portable television, and the radio that picks up TV audio. It used to be that a set was a piece of furniture. Today, there are models that can fit into a large handbag, and the radios can fit into a good-sized pocket. A person on the go can at least hear a program almost any place. Given the involvement of the soap fan, there's every reason to believe that thousands are not letting work, shopping, or anything else get in the way of their favorite soaps. It's a known fact that some soap viewers who move only about the house keep extra portables and/or radio in strategic locations so that nothing, absolutely nothing, causes them to miss a line.

The fact is that soap devotees are not like other television viewers. They don't simply "watch" a show; they live with it—live with its characters year after year. Some fans take the soaps in their lives with great seriousness—like the woman who wrote to a fan magazine, "I really enjoy viewing them with extreme anxiety(!)." Others see the shows as campy humor. But even these fans are involved. Some ask (or pay) friends to watch a show that they will have to miss. Others (superfans, students with irregular schedules, and people who must be out of the country) subscribe to newsletters and magazines that provide plot summaries. A dedicated fan will accept few excuses from the networks for preempting a soap. When *Somerset* was interrupted by news from the '76 Republican National Convention, about 350 people in Washington, D.C., alone called in to protest.

Actors and actresses in particular can attest to fan involvement. Many of the leading performers have fan clubs that publish journals, disseminate T-shirts, etc. Those actors who don't have clubs are likely to be inundated by all sorts of messages and tokens anyway. They get fan letters, advice or rebukes (mainly for their characters), and when they or their characters have birthdays, weddings, babies, etc., they may receive baskets full of good wishes and hundreds of dollars worth of gifts. Some stars are the objects of near-worship. Every weekday, high school girls gather at the doors of ABC's *All My Children* studios, hoping to catch one of the romantic heroes. And one young man declared that if he could get close enough to his favorite heroine, "they'd have to scrape me off her with razor blades."

Many fans feel so involved with a particular character that they "lobby" on his or her behalf, sometimes influencing the storyline. In no other television genre does fan involvement mean so much. Letters to writers and producers can mean changes in plot or the death knell for a character. "The audience is a paramount consideration in daytime," says one associate producer who feels that the rapport between the audience and the show is much stronger than on night-time programs. "When we get letters, not only are they all answered personally....but [they] are reproduced so that they can be discussed at the next story meeting." The producers, writers, and directors of the soaps don't do this as a public relations gimmick. They have genuine respect for the opinions and the wishes of soap viewers. The shows, one should add, haven't been hurt as a result of audience input. Soaps maintain high standards of integrity and professionalism, and they are in fact better acted and produced now than they were in the past.

Soaps are an example of the media giving the public exactly what it wants: good stories, good acting and good production values. Most of the fourteen soaps now on the air are flourishing. (How many night-time shows have lasted twenty years or more? Several soaps have.) In fact, the soaps are doing better than ever since soap watching has become the thing to do. Every day, people across the country are immersing themselves in the soap operatic brew of love, sex, talk, and human turmoil. After more than 40 years, soap opera is finally a story in itself, and Americans have come to admit that they love it.

THE NEW SOAP GENERATION

2

Item: It has been reported that at noon each day a large number of students at Princeton University emerge from their classrooms and seek the nearest available television sets. With august works of science, philosophy, history, and literature still cradled in their arms, they watch *The Young and the Restless,* one of the most popular programs on campus.

Item: Last year a 17-year-old girl who found herself overwhelmed by emotional problems took the unusual step of telephoning actress Fran Heflin (Mona Kane, *All My Children*). Another mother and daughter wrote Miss Heflin a joint letter stating that they had not been getting along, but had watched the show together, and now had a basis from which to begin discussing their problems.

Item: At the spring 1976 meeting of Alpha Psi Omega sororities, women throughout New England voted Tony Craig (*Edge of Night*) "the daytime actor we'd most like to spend a night time with." Wrote the president of Alpha Psi, "We will not miss a day of *The Edge of Night* as long as the best looking young man on television is on the show!"

Item: When students at Duke University were asked why they watch soaps, one replied, "It's the only constant in our lives."

On college campuses across America, soap opera has suddenly become the "in thing." Between the hours of 11 a.m. and 4:30 p.m., television lounges are filled with soap opera fans. These college students know the plots as well as any other ardent fans, and soap personalities are among their heroes. The latest doings of the Brooks sisters et al., are recounted in hallways where not long ago political rhetoric was the order of things. A couple years ago if students mentioned "Nixon," they meant Richard. Now there's a fair chance that they're talking about Agnes.

Actually soaps are more than a college fad; they're a youth fad generally. High school students may have more difficulty watching the programs because of their restricted schedules, but their love of soap opera is documented by the Nielsen figures. When school is out, the ratings for some shows jump by as many as 9 points (which is worth about 9 million dollars to the networks). After vacation, say early September, there is an equally drastic drop. Though young

Producer John Conboy started the trend of the new generation with *The Young and the Restless.* Here he chats with the actress who plays Peggy Brooks.

Guiding Light is one of the oldest soaps on the air, but it too has incorporated young characters, such as Eve Stapleton (left), and story lines with appeal to a new generation of viewers. Lew Dancy (right) is another youth-oriented character.

working people have even more restricted hours, they too are soap enthusiasts. One young working woman admitted that she turned down a higher paying job rather than giving up watching her favorite serials. According to a network survey, more than 70% of all women under 19 years of age prefer serials to other types of daytime programming.

Of course young people have always watched some soap opera. Back in the 1960s, a group of Boston University students arranged their class schedules so that they could be free to watch *One Life to Live* everyday. But that was uncommon then. Most college students dismissed soap opera out of hand. The label was pejorative. If, for instance, someone said that a book was like a soap opera, it was understood to be a put down. Then again, the sixties were a vastly different time. The constant in a student's life was the Viet Nam War, and that dominated discussion and thought. Talk of great moment and high seriousness prevailed.

At the present time, seriousness has been replaced by the gospel of fun. Tom Wolfe summed up current campus attitudes this way: "Life keeps getting easier, sunnier, happier…Frisbee!" Kathy Glass, the young actress who plays Jenny (*One Life to Live*), found that that sentiment is common in high schools as well. On a tour of schools around the country, she discovered that young people were "sick of this 'sturm and drang' business. They wanted some happiness, to be happy."

It may seem contradictory that young people wanting happiness should turn to a genre that is known for its portrayal of trouble. But soap opera is enjoyment. That is, the romantic stories of Phil and Tara, Jenny and Tim, and Liza and Steve are clearly more fun than the progress of foreign policy or civil rights legislation. The soap opera character, like the college-age viewer, is searching for more happy happy love, and probably not finding it. She is not, by contrast, searching for a theory of art, an honest mayor, an integrated neighborhood, and not finding *that*. Unlike the issues-oriented "in" activities of the sixties, the soap opera fulfills fun-fantasy needs. And it provides what every young person dearly wants in life—a chance to feel close to people without having to bear any responsibility for all that goes wrong with them.

Some young people take the soaps as pure fun and low camp; they follow a show mainly to delight in the corny complications. Others take the shows seriously, as models for solving life problems. This apparently does not diminish the enjoyment. As an 18-year-old from Nebraska said, "I care about the people. Their problems are yours. You relate to them." But she doesn't relate to them in a deeply emotional way. She watches, she says, "Just for fun. It's escapism."

No matter how they see the soaps, young people are watching in record numbers. This in itself has altered soap opera. The most obvious change is in the age of the characters. "It seems they're getting rid of all my favorite characters and bringing in all these new young kids," complained one long-time viewer. And it's a valid complaint. Until recently, middle-aged characters were in control of major storylines. "Young people" on serials were in their late twenties and early thirties. Usually they were young marrieds, and the problems they faced related to the domestic scene. Young viewers had virtually no peers to identify with. If they identified at all, it was through older characters who might have reminded them of their parents.

Then, six years ago, *All My Children* introduced a pair of truly young lovers—still in high school! Though it was a daring move, it had little effect on soap opera as a whole. Problems of middle age still far outnumbered those of adolescence.

The real leader in the youth movement was *The Young and the Restless* which came breathlessly on the scene shortly afterward. Suddenly a soap opera was showing not simply adolescent subplot, but more young faces than had been seen on daytime television since American Bandstand. The story revolved around youth in the form of the Brooks sisters, who ranged in age from late teens to early twenties. (One of them, Peggy Brooks, is still in college.) In fact the show was so youth-oriented that even the adults tended to look like adolescents. It was a youth soap if there ever was one; and it was a hit especially with the young and the restless in the audience. By the end of 1975, it was number 4 in the daytime Nielsens. Today it has the best rating in the critical 18- 34-year-old group.

Success in television is a prophesy of sorts and sure enough *The Young and the Restless* augured a new direction in daytime drama.

Young viewers (like their parents and grandparents) are interested in story lines about romance; young romance is typified by Penny Davis and Jerry Dancy in *The Doctors* (left). On youth-oriented soaps, such as *Ryan's Hope,* the plot goes one step farther and introduces sex. The courtship of Mary Ryan by the man she eventually married, Jack Fenelli, bordered on "mature subject matter."

Virtually all the other shows began killing off the old folks and adding young people in bunches. *Search for Tomorrow,* the oldest soap, seemed to have commandeered a school bus and hired everyone on board except the driver. Most amusing was the rapid aging process that hit soapland. Overnight, infants ripened into pubescent teenagers brimming with sexual energy and ready to go out and get into trouble. The net result of this has been that all shows have at least a few characters between the ages of 15-25 who are central figures in the drama. Whether young people identify with these characters isn't ascertainable. But they can identify with the situations young characters find themselves in—conflicts with parents, career-identity crises, first loves, etc. The result is that college students find the soaps more immediate, more meaningful.

Producers and writers are trying to make soaps more "meaningful" to young people in another sense: by dealing with social issues they think are of concern to them. Women's liberation questions are especially prominent. When Rachel Cory (*Another World*) decided to pursue a career in sculpture, there were suddenly strains in her marriage that have continued to be of consequence. How this is resolved is thought to be of great interest to young viewers. Other social issues on today's soaps include interracial dating, the effect of divorce on teenage children, abortion and single motherhood, teenage prostitution, and drugs. While there is some question as to whether these youth-oriented issues really attract viewers—Glass found that young people mostly wanted romantic love scenes—they have a certain public relations value. And they have occasionally legitimized political or social views. For example Ruth Martin's polemic against war legitimized some young people's stand on Viet Nam. The speech, though mild, even banal in its language, provoked considerable audience response. In any case, social issues seem to have become ingrained in, or at least tacked onto, the genre.

This is not to suggest that soaps have become political, message-oriented, or excessively preachy. Social issues usually are presented on the level that all other soap opera matters are presented: the emotional level. Soap characters traditionally have not been analytic types. They have tended to feel rather than figure out, and to a large

8

The trials and tribulations of young love, exemplified by Kevin and Phoebe Jamison (right) on *Edge of Night*, are a staple of the soaps. The longest running cliff hanger is the romance of Tara and Phil Brent (left) on *All My Children*.

extent that is still so. But to appeal to young viewers, writers have made some changes there too. Periodically some contemporary-sounding, psychologically or spiritually discerning voices can be heard. For example, young characters will lapse into the lingo of pop psychoanalyses. "It wasn't real love," a character proclaimed recently. "It was neurotic dependence." Additional contemporary voices include a number of knowing psychiatrists, a mod clergyman, a family planner, *and* a guitar-playing free-lance religious type who strolls through the set of *The Young and the Restless* preaching about love and self-esteem.

Comparing a soap opera of 15 years ago with today's versions, one will be struck by another effect of the youth movement. Soaps *look* younger, and it's not simply due to youthful characters. The shows themselves have been given a face lift of sorts: they have become stylish and up-to-date. Young and old alike sport clothes and hair styles that jetsetters wouldn't be ashamed to be seen in. Even old-line characters have not been able to resist modernization; on *Love of Life* for example, Vanessa (Audrey Peters) was finally ordered to cut off her french twist. Settings and decor have also become more fashionable. Until recently, characters ventured out of the kitchen or the living room only to go on trial, have an operation, or be run over by a truck. Now bars, discotheques, to say nothing of places like Odyssey House, are featured. Dowdiness has been banished; glamor is the order of the day.

Content, as well as style, tends to favor the trendsetting young. In particular, today's soaps are less hesitant about portraying sexual feelings and behaviors. Though sex has been a fact of soap life for some time, before the youth movement its only evidence was an announcement of pregnancy. The cameras stopped discreetly at the bedroom door (unless of course someone was dying inside). Today's newest soap, *Ryan's Hope,* has shown young couples in bed. They only talk and kiss to be sure, but it's a lot sexier and the implications are a lot clearer than they used to be. Other soaps, too, are making use of the bedroom. *The Young and the Restless,* for one, frequently indicates that pillow talk and what follows is not an insignificant part of marriage. Most soaps are trying to be more up-front and honest about the idea of sex, an attitude which young people appreciate.

The new youth orientation has definitely made the soaps sexier. Both unmarried (Trish Clayton and Mike Horton, *Days of Our Lives,* left) and married (Jeff and Monica Webber, *General Hospital,* right) couples have more daring love scenes than were ever seen a decade ago.

Young viewers can also appreciate the ways soaps depict young romance. Though skeptical older characters may put it down, the programs themselves do not. Young couples may have sex, may even live together before marriage, but none of this is ever sensationalized or cheapened. These relationships are taken as seriously as couplings in the older generations, and, what must be particularly satisfying to a young audience, young and old have similar problems.

Though young viewers may identify primarily with young characters and the situations they find themselves in, they are fans of some of the older characters as well. In several of them, they have found attractive role models. Characters like Mona Kane (*All My Children*) and Maeve Ryan (*Ryan's Hope*) are two favorites. Both are older women who are sympathetic, wise, and understanding. Given that they are rather plain, unglamorous figures, their popularity with the young is remarkable. Actress Fran Heflin who plays Mona, was the center of an appreciative riot when she visited her daughter on campus. Many young people regard her as a "favorite aunt" or perhaps the mother they wish they had. Other characters are appreciated for the opposite reason: Phoebe Tyler (*All My Children*) interests young viewers because she is snobbish, deceitful, in short a caricature of what they object to in their parents' generation.

That characters are perceived as good or bad presupposes that a value system underlies soap opera characterizations. In fact, this value system is one that is particularly attractive to young people. It is fiercely honest. The worst sin in the afternoon is the willingness to lie for personal advantage. Deception is the mark of the villain, and it is of course what young people dislike above all—particularly in their elders.

In the soaps, the one act that is consistently condemned is lying. "You always end up hurting someone," says a character in *Days of Our Lives*. That includes lying to protect someone's feelings, lying to keep up appearances, and lying "for the good of the children." There is no valid reason for deceit in soap opera. Dishonesty ruins relationships, particularly relationships between parents and children. (I'm trying to love you," says one young heroine to her mother, "but all the lies get in the way.") Misguided, dishonest

compassion is no compassion, the soaps seem to say. It is a hard-nosed, relatively unsugared view that many young people share.

Another bias of contemporary soap opera thought to reflect the values of the young is the implied anti-materialism, or at least anti-wealth, on many shows. Older women with money are almost by definition villains. When one appears, it's inevitable that she will try to buy off someone's lover or potential lover. After lying, this is the worst serial evil. In the soap opera philosophy of today, "emotions can't be dictated to," much less purchased. Yet there are people who try. Even male characters, usually a harmless if not benevolent bunch, are prone to abuse the power of wealth. Rich bachelors are the worst, often trying to manipulate the young or innocent with money that is ill-gotten to begin with. The only exceptions to the anti-wealth prejudices of soap opera are the family men who inherit money, like Bucky Carter (*Ryan's Hope*) or Chuck Tyler (*All My Children*). They are good men on whom fortune has smiled, and they smile back.

The soap opera's insistence upon honesty in personal relationships, and its suspicion of wealth are two attitudes that appeal to young people. But perhaps the principal appeal is that soap operas are hard-nosed in their attempt to show the difficulties of life and love. There are no easy answers in daytime drama. Much of the philosophy that emerges reflects the emotional mind-set of young people growing up and discovering the nature of things. "I remember praying as a little boy that nothing bad would ever happen to the people we love," a character on *As the World Turns* remarked. "We grow up and become realistic, but we can't help hoping." As every college-age person finds out, bad things happen to people *because* they love. "Caring deeply—it does trip us up sometimes, doesn't it," a female character says typically. She sounds like any thoughtful young person who has newly entered the world of adult relationships. Indeed, one of the "messages" of soap operas is that hurting is a part of life. A character on *Ryan's Hope*, sounding like the refrain of a country-western song, says, "Learning is painful; growing is painful; loving is painful. But there's one thing you can say about pain: when you're feeling it you know you're alive." It's the lesson of young adulthood.

Many young viewers identify with the character Jenny Wolek Siegel on *One Life to Live*. Kathy Glass, the actress who plays Jenny, has toured the country to speak to her fans in high schools.

Finally, the soaps do more than provide attractive models and philosophies to young people. They offer *social* reassurance: they say that, contrary to the what we hear from other media, ours is not a world of singles bars and cynicism. Indeed, soaps are a countervailing voice in what Benjamin De Mott describes as a "permissive, sexually liberated, 'nonrepressive' society," a society in which we are hounded daily by porn and border porn, by X and marginal X, R, PG, by the universal tide of knowingness that tugs and nudges, thickens the air, loosens the principles, mucks up every good act by reminding it of its exceptionality." The soaps are a countervailing force in that they provide young people with storylines and ambiance that reflect old-fashioned, down-home social values. It's an uncorrupted world in which marriage is made much of and the dirtiest thing that happens is a lie.

Do young people really want these old-fashioned values, those sterling grandmothers on their porches, those misguided heroines stumbling in and out of churches? Will they really take the countless love affairs and marriages of Julie Olsen Banning Anderson Williams over one good Open Marriage?

According to Kathy Glass, they will indeed. On her tour of high schools, Miss Glass discovered that young fans aren't looking for explicit sex or promiscuous characters. Chastity and other beliefs thought by social observers to have gone out with the pill, are important to them. They want marriage and they want families. Glass was particularly interested in learning about the attitudes of young fans toward recent social trends. She passed out a questionnaire that included an item, "A lot of people say that marriage is obsolete, what do you think?" The response was unanimous. "Down to the last one, they said…'Marriage is a sacred institution,' or 'I'm going to get married,' or 'that's not true, marriage is very important.'" And she added that they regard living together as "wrong, wrong, wrong!"

The soaps reassure these young viewers. The shows may deal with "sex," but it is always supposed to be serious, which means oriented toward eventual marriage. Promiscuity or casual sex of any kind is frowned upon. Heroines may have sex outside marriage if they are deeply in love and anticipate marriage; but just as often

These young fans have just had the thrill of watching the taping of their favorite show, *All My Children*.

young women are unrepentant virgins "saving themselves for marriage" as the saying goes. Chris Brooks of the trendiest youth soap, *The Young and the Restless*, found out a while back that her boyfriend was sleeping with another girl. (Among other old-fashioned things, there's still something of a double standard on serials.) Chris, in anger, decided to give Snapper "the same thing Sally had given him." Then poised at the brink, she backed off, unable to go through with it, and Snapper said *he respected her for it!* Chris' attitude was hardly trendy, perhaps even "out of it." But it was vintage soap opera. Good, straight heroines, from the beginning of radio serials, stumbled chastely along to marriage with the most handsome, eligible men in town—and they still do. This is in sharp contrast to nighttime television and films. There, heroines and heroes have a much more casual attitude toward sex, and they are usually attractive enough to "score" with just about anybody they please. On a steady diet of that, a viewer almost has to feel socially backward. Young people who are just beginning their adult social lives are perhaps more vulnerable to those feelings, and they find soaps' images reassuring. In fact, Kathy Glass discovered that many young people identified with her character (Jenny) precisely because she is "out of it." "All those people leaning to 'squarenessville' [a word itself about 15 years out of date], you know would really identify with her—because you could be good and follow your parents' advice and still make out."

On the basis of her tour, Glass was asked what kind of soap opera she would write for young people. She replied, "I would stay away from careers and social issues. I would get more into sex and romance and who's marrying whom." On one hand, she has a point. It was for the stories of love and romance that young people started watching. (Soaps changed after they began watching, not vice versa.) On the other hand, those shows that have added young people, that have tried to speak more to the young, that have added new ideas, and have confronted social issues, are the soaps that young viewers tend to watch. It is that fact which continues to spur the youth movement in daytime drama. We are likely to see more of it in the years ahead: younger characters and younger viewers will certainly bring more change.

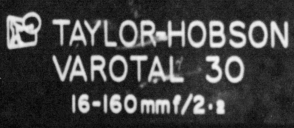

SOAP APPEAL

3

In recent years, some critics have begun to notice "improvements" in daytime drama. Faces are younger, sets more varied, and sex more explicit. Moreover, storylines are "relevant"—at least on some shows. *All My Children* with its adventures in Viet Nam, *The Young and the Restless* with its depiction of breast cancer, are among the shows and episodes singled out for praise. Soaps like *As the World Turns*, meanwhile, are criticized for being too traditional, unadventurous, and unrealistic.

Fans, however, don't seem to care. For years millions have watched soaps without regard to critical opinions. *As the World Turns* is a case in point. It is one of the leaders of the daytime Nielsens and has been since the 1950s. Even on the so-called "improved" soaps, producers seldom get letters from fans complaining about traditional turns in the story. In fact, it's fair to say that people like and want the old soap operatic elements: the amnesia, the mysterious babies, and all that. These elements are in part what distinguish soap opera from other forms, and therefore they must relate strongly to its appeal. Yet the old soap opera conventions are said to be laughably unrealistic, and grounds for dismissing the genre altogether.

Soap opera imitating soap opera

Now no art form is wholly realistic; each is unrealistic in its own way—in ways that meet the needs or express the feelings of the audience. It follows that no art form can be condemned simply for being "unrealistic." To look at an abstract painting and criticize it because it does not resemble a tree or house or any concrete object would not be intelligent, or fair. Nor would it be fair to criticize a Nineteenth Century novel for not investigating sexual intercourse or bodily eliminations, both of which must certainly go on in the lives of its characters.

If we accept soap opera as a form of art, however minor or "popular," then we cannot criticize it for not showing us life as it is. It is thoroughly surprising that critics fall into the trap of doing so— that they go on and on about the preponderance of doctors, the peculiarity of pregnancies, the naivete of small town white Anglo Saxon settings, etc., etc. It would be more fair, and more enlightening, to look at the unrealistic elements in soap opera as we do the abstraction in a modern painting, or the prudery in an old-fashioned novel. What, we might ask, does the presence of these unrealistic elements say about us, and to us? Or, to be broader than that: How does the material of soap opera, both realistic and unrealistic, satisfy the inner needs of those who watch?

> *The fantasy of everyday (every-single-day) romance*

Soap operas are primarily fantasies of romance. They are set not in Medieval days, or colonial days, or Civil War days, but within the context of the most ordinary, everyday life. In the kitchen, even. The soap fulfills the viewer's need to feel (if not believe) that the business of life is romantic courtship—never anything too grand or heroic (never anything that approaches Nineteenth Century Romanticism) but courtship nonetheless. Such courtship hardly ends with marriage. It doesn't end at all, except insofar as life itself ends, at the hands of Fate.

What attracts us to soap opera characters is the luxurious way in which they manage their relationships. Soap characters don't simply have romances; they *live* romances. Unrealistically they shove aside the common details of life ("milkmen, laundrymen and exterminators never intrude into the immaculate living rooms of the Brookses or Grants or Chancellors," writes one critic). Doctors spend more time operating on their love lives than operating. Child care is no trouble at all. Successful and presumably hardworking business men and women have unlimited time to discuss interpersonal relationships. It seems that romance-related activities overwhelm everyone except a few wise old patriarchs and matriarchs. And if this isn't fantasy enough—it all happens within what appear to be perfectly ordinary middle-class homes.

The soap opera omits the common business of life for the same reason the Nineteenth Century novel omitted sex: it doesn't relate to the fantasy needs of the audience, and it is not acceptable material in the genre anyhow. Like other romantic fiction, the soaps are written not to be realistic but to impart a fantasy. In the soaps, the fantasy is that there is no such thing as getting in a rut: lives are, to use actor John Reilly's phrase, always "hotting up." No one is ever settled or put away. Some of the more obvious conventions of soap opera are really only proof of this. Critics have noted, for example, that widowhood is a short-term phenomenon. Usually a widow has a suitor even before her unfortunate husband is run over or crashes into something fatally. If by any chance she doesn't, some suitor will emerge almost at once. Similarly, women married for years suddenly find new love affairs. Maybe their husbands have wandered off—amnesia's the usual reason—just in time for suitors from the past to reappear. Or maybe it's just some simple infidelity. No matter the circumstance. Nothing precludes the re-entry of romance. For people in the audience who are in a rut, or fear falling into one (and that includes most everyone), the soap opera formula is reassuring. If your life is now routine-respectable, where nothing ever "hots up" except the stove or the iron, don't worry. It's just temporary.

> *The romantic fantasy of sex*

The treatment of sex, ancillary to all this romance, also meets specific fantasy needs. The people who watch the soaps are not old-fashioned or naive; they know as much as anyone about new sexual lifestyles, erotic marriage manuals and casual sex. But this doesn't stop them from watching soap operas that romanticize, or minimize sexuality. Most soap operas are sexually unrealistic. They appeal to the still-present need in most of us to see sex the way our grandparents did—which means with eyes half closed. This has little to do with actual lifestyles, or the stimulation viewers might seek from other media.

Soaps differ in the amount of sexual activity they can show. But the audience needs that are played to are pretty constant. There is no noncommital sex, no hip sex, no sex for sex's sake (a striking difference from other popular media). There is no raunchy fun sex on the traditional shows (and even on the newer shows it's left to the unsympathetic characters). Sex is not usually a motive for romance; nor does romance necessarily lead to a sexual relationship. (If it leads to anything, it leads to marriage or endless frustration in pursuit of marriage.) Of course, as the illegitimate birth rate indicates, there's a fair amount of sex anyway. But here again, the portrayal is in line with what we have tended to see as the feminine romantic fantasy. There are no realistic physical details, no discussion of the act, and no preparation for its consequences.

Though some passion is generally indicated, it is not a matter of importance whether or not intercourse took place. A kind of wishful womanly ambiguity surrounds the actual events. (And writers feel that ambiguity leaves more options in the direction of the story, for example, possibilities like, "I'm giving him up before it gets too serious," or "I'm pregnant.") Certainly sex is not confronted as an issue prior to the act. Mature adults rarely concern themselves with matters of contraception. All this offends the critics, who point to the unrealistically high incidence of surprise pregnancies on the soaps. Yet this conforms to the old-fashioned need we sometimes have to believe that sex is naturally romantic and magic—not something we anticipate with diaphragms, not something we work at, or for that matter, have fun at.

Soap operas argue that love and sex are mostly a verbal phenomenon. (There is some evidence that this is true—that for women, words really are the greatest turn on. No mind: this is another area in which soaps are said to be unrealistic, hence offensive.) Dr. Dan Stewart (*As the World Turns*) confesses to Kim

Dixon that he loves her before he's even kissed her. Ruth Martin (*All My Children*), though soundly married, suddenly inspires articulate declarations of love. Cupid's arrow seems to strike most characters in the tongue. Words count more than any action. People are obsessed with hearing them. Men, who tend on the soaps to be insecure, will say things like, "I want to hear that you love me," which is apparently what the audience also wants. Men will make exquisite differentiations between the love they feel for one woman as compared to another, or for the same woman at different times. Especially on older soaps, a great deal of time is consumed by characters merely deciding whether or not to express their feelings. All this caters to the feminine need to hear words, words, words of love from a male population seldom so articulate in this or any other area of human relationships. The emphasis on emotional language, and the minimization of physical or casual sex are conventions one can easily ridicule. But they fulfill fantasy needs not met by other contemporary forms.

> *The romantic fantasy of children*

The same might be said about conventions surrounding the presentation of children. Many critics have complained that there are only cute and mysteriously born infants, and teenage children—that "overnight they turn into voting age monsters." (*Time* Magazine). This is usually explained as a practical ploy on the part of directors, or idiocy on the part of the writers. No attention has been given to the needs which this unrealistic picture satisfies. Bearing children can be romantic, and having grown children requires little time. But in the intervening years, ages 1-15, parenthood is time-consuming and often difficult. (Parents never fantasize about *those* years; they never wonder what it will be like when their child is eight, but there is endless speculation about what a child will be "when he grows up.") Soaps simply translate the parental fantasy into drama. Children are brought home from the hospital, are sent upstairs, and then are either forgotten or re-emerge a couple of years later fully grown. There are some exceptions: children will occasionally appear as dramatic devices, that is to complicate romantic or domestic situations. Six-year-old Phil Tyler (*All My Children*) was always mentioned as the main obstacle to Tara and Phil's marriage (though, conveniently, he tended to spend most of his time at "Timmy's"). Young Tommy Hobart (*General Hospital*) had to be shielded from the alcoholic rampages of his stepfather. And children like Betsy Stewart (*As the World Turns*) do sometimes help place in perspective the love affairs of their parents. But these cases are exceptions. For the most part, school-age children are neither seen nor heard. They represent objective responsibilities and the audience in fantasy wants to be free of them.

As we can see, romance is the foundation and rationale of the soap opera storyline. It explains the absence of children, the absence of birth control, and a number of other unrealistic soap tendencies. However, the way in which a story will be worked out—what will happen from day to day—is another matter. There are things that almost never happen either because of convention (no lesbianism) or because of the upper middle-class environment of the soap opera (few poor blacks). On the other hand, there are a number of incidents that always seem to happen. Among them are some of the genre's least realistic moments—some of the material that best satisfies audience fantasies in the afternoon.

> *The fantasy of the newly-discovered parent*

One typical and unbelievable incident is the hero's discovery of a new and unsuspected parent. On shows like *Days of Our Lives,* there is hardly a character who has not had (or cannot look forward to) this unusual experience. In the soaps, people are not stuck with their parents. They can find new ones. If this seldom happens in real life, it does happen in fantasy. Many psychologists have pointed out that the identity crisis typically involves fantasies of acquiring new sets of parents. The teenage child imagines that his parents are not his real parents. Perhaps, as in a fairy tale, they are a king and queen, a politician or film star. Or conversely, they may be villains. The possibilities are at once exciting and fearsome.

In the real world, parents losing track of their children (or vice versa) is hardly an everyday event. Losing both parents "seems like carelessness," says the literal-minded Lady Bracknell in Oscar Wilde's "The Importance of Being Earnest." But on the soaps losing track of one or both parents is a way of life. People regularly discover that they have new or additional fathers and mothers. Secrets of infidelity and illegitimacy lie smoldering for years only to be abruptly revealed by a jealous rival or a blood test taken at a fatal moment. Sometimes the character finds out that the new parent is worse than the original one; other times better. The results are unimportant. The fact that the fantasy is satisfying keeps it fresh from year to year, and show to show.

> *The amnesia fantasy*

This is also true of the classic soap fantasy: amnesia. Even fond viewers of the soaps are quick to make fun of the near epidemic of memory loss—and, looking at it from a realistic point of view, it *is* absurd. Amnesia isn't that uncommon as a shock reaction, as thousands of people who've been in accidents can testify. However, shock reactions seldom last more than a few hours, do not involve loss of identity, and do not lead to new lives.

In fantasy, a brief shock reaction means little, while the chance to start a new life is tremendously intriguing. Anyone who has felt current hassles growing oppressive has thought wistfully of becoming someone else. Actually, people *can* walk out on their lives. Doing it willfully, though, would be an evasion of responsibilities. It would mean leaving children without a parent, parents without a child, and general hardship and anguish to many. Having amnesia, on the other hand, means literally "never having to say you're sorry" because you don't even know who you're supposed to be saying it to. The amnesiac is freed simultaneously of problems and guilt, and as an added benefit, gains sympathy for the exquisite horror of having forgotten everything.

Soap characters regularly experience total amnesia and/or "protective" memory blocks. When Amanda (*Days of Our Lives*) enters the hospital with a brain tumor, she is involved in a complex triangle with a pair of doctors. Upon coming out of the anesthetic, she discovers that the thoughtful surgeons excised her memory along with her tumor. Her suitors are there by her side unselfishly caring for her while she tries to recall incidents of her childhood. Less traumatic perhaps but also effective was Kim Dixon's amnesia experience (*As the World Turns*). A benevolent tornado robbed her of the memory that she loved Dr. Dan Stewart and that she didn't love her husband. Escape from her problems was easy, if temporary. Probably every person watching was able to relate to it, though each knew that he would never experience anything like it. Amnesia may be clinically bizarre, but it is really only an extreme interpretation of a recurring soap fantasy—that people can start "a whole new life" in which the mistakes of the past play no part. (The invitation to do this is one of the most common lines in soapland.)

Amnesia, of course, is only one medical problem that is portrayed in a way that fulfills audience fantasies. The soaps are full of sickness and death (though, as we shall see, the two are not related). Physical conditions in general are so tied up with romance and wishful thinking that they seldom bear any semblance to reality. Producers seem very worried about portraying medical problems realistically, for fear that this will upset viewers. In consequence, since radio days, characters have faced one fanciful medical situation after another. Indeed they sometimes seem to have alien physiologies—for no human could experience things the ways they experience them. For example, in the medical wing of soap opera, pregnancy is one condition that is really fearful. Disease and death, though, are consistently portrayed in ways that soothe viewer fears.

> *Fantasies*
> *of*
> *pregnancy*

This unrealistic picture has attracted considerable attention. For example, Rose Goldsen, in *Human Behavior,* reports on the "kinds of images" that soap opera produced during the first half of 1975—and does she seem dismayed!

> Eleven pregnancies produced two miscarriages, two abortions under consideration, two births almost fatal to the mother, a third premature delivery that took place during a blizzard without qualified medical assistance. [The soaps] lost only one mother in the year's first half. That was poor Addie Williams who died just after being delivered of baby Hope, who survived. Addie died not of the terminal cancer she was suffering from, nor from the complications to be expected when a grandmother goes through pregnancy. She was killed in a car accident. (*Days of Our Lives*)

What is to be said about these images—aside from the obvious point that they are unique to soap opera?

First, we might recognize that pregnancy as portrayed in the soaps is not a physical condition, but a romantic ordeal. The course of pregnancy is not influenced by the techniques of modern medicine, but by the more backward workings of the heart. Feelings of mother, father, and uncomfortable third parties affect the conception as well as the outcome. This is reflected in the language used: for example, Anne (*All My Children*) says at one point, "Our baby was conceived in love and will be born in love and there's no way it can be less than perfect." She makes that declaration in the face of hard medical evidence that her baby may be infected with a disease that causes mental retardation.

If the pregnant woman has a need to think of her baby in these romantic terms—and there is evidence that she does—then the soaps play this out in dialogue, and of course in plot.

Most striking are the fear fantasies that surround miscarriages. A significant number of miscarriages are induced by the misbehavior of the father-to-be. For example, Steve Frame is married to good-character Alice, who is pregnant. Steve sneaks off to see his evil ex-lover Rachel (and his child by her) and Alice immediately has a miscarriage (*Another World*). Again, newly married Chris Foster discovers she is pregnant with husband Snapper's child. Shortly thereafter she discovers that Sally is also pregnant with her husband's child. Chris loses the baby (*Young and Restless*). Phyllis Curtis loses her baby merely because her husband comes home drunk (*Days of Our Lives*). The fear-fantasy being acted out in these and similar instance is clear: "You play around, and I'll get sick and lose the baby and it will be your fault."

A related fantasy dictates that a female rival may also "cause" a miscarriage (or premature delivery). Through means too complicated to be reported or believed, it is made clear that Iris caused Rachel's miscarriage (*Another World*), and Brooke caused Julie's (*Days of Our Lives*). The writers really have to work hard to come up with a storyline that justifies these conclusions (after all, one woman cannot cause a miscarriage in another, short of physical violence). But it is an important fear-fantasy, and allows the heroine and her fans to blame miscarriages (potential or actual) on ill-wishers. This is something women can do only in fantasy—and on the soaps.

Once we accept pregnancy as a romantic ordeal, the reason for many miscarriages becomes clear. For example, we can see why the woman who wrongly marries a man to "give her baby a name" will often be rewarded with a miscarriage (that's what happened to Erica and Kitty, *All My Children,* and Kim, *As the World Turns,* in past storylines). And it's clear too why a wronged woman, denied marriage, goes on to deliver a healthy baby. Clarice (*Another World*) and Jill Foster (*Young and Restless*) are examples of this type.

Sometimes, of course, a miscarriage represents a change of heart on the part of the writer; and some troubled pregnancies are nothing but suspense. But soap pregnancies in general are an acting out of feminine fear-fantasies, and perfectly valid in those terms. (Even the high incidences of pregnancy following one night of passion plays on a common fear-fantasy—a fear formed many years before the pill, and one which cannot be emotionally updated).

*F*antasies
of
death

Medical conditions other than pregnancy are presented in a way to undermine adult fears of mortality. Cancer is cured at an unbelievable rate, and paralysis comes and goes just long enough for a character to become sympathetic. These and other physical problems are pictured much in the way children imagine them. Children wonder what it would be like to be unable to walk for a while, or what it would mean to be blind. As a test, they might try walking down the street eyes closed. Soap characters seem to do the same. After a couple episodes of transiting around in a wheelchair or resigning themselves to a sightless life, they suddenly walk or see again.

The portrayal of death is, in all, comforting. Critics make much of the high body count on your ordinary soap, as if this were enough to frighten or depress a reasonable viewer. They fail to notice that death in the soaps appeals to childhood fear-fantasies, which are relatively non-threatening compared to what we learn as adults.

Children are afraid of being run over by trucks, eaten by animals, or shot at by robbers and cowboys. But they are not aware of the slow physical suffering that comes with debilitating illness and old age. In a fearful child's world, people die not because they are sick or old—but because they are unlucky or bad. And this is what happens in the soaps. The afore-mentioned Addie Hamilton does not die because she has terminal cancer, or has delivered a baby very late in life (adult fears); instead, having survived all this, she is run over by a truck (child's fear). Mary Kennicott (*All My Children*) dies not from a recurrence of leukemia (adult fear); once cured, she is killed by a crazed gunman whom she unwisely lets into her home (child's fear). There *is* a high body count in soapland, but it's not very threatening, since most viewers cannot sit around worrying about the ill luck manifested in gunmen and trucks. Statistically speaking, the soaps are so unrealistic in their chosen forms of death that chronic patients in nursing homes can, and do, watch without being threatened by the constant killing off of characters.

As everyone in the storyline business knows, characters are not supposed to die of any disease which members of the audience might be dying of (which is another way of saying that disease and death are not to be presented in a threatening, realistic way). To avoid the problem of audience identification, studios make up diseases with names like Melinkoff, Extra-Vascular Supplementary Propensity (ESP), and Abonda Fever. When Abonda Fever struck *The Doctors* a few years ago several viewers wrote in to say that they had it. The show responded, "No you don't, because we made it up." (Trust us not to come up with something you might actually die of!) As in a child's world, disease is virtually unrelated to death. So is old age (the young die as frequently as the old). As for the hospital, it's a place for romantic intrigue—not for dying.

There is one more reason that death in the soap opera is non-threatening—maybe even satisfying to some viewers. While death in the real world is inexplicable and seemingly arbitrary, death in soap opera is perfectly understandable. Death is swift, guided by the hands of Fate (from the story's point of view) or the hands of the writers (from the insider/fan point of view). The metaphor of death is usually a truck (a plane, car, staircase or precipitous ledge will also do); it rumbles down on villains certainly, unpopular characters inevitably, and good people if they're being written out of the show. On rare occasions a quick illness will take a character; for example, Grandpa Hughes died quickly of old age when the actor did (*As the World Turns*). But usually death strikes for reasons having little to do with like events in the real world. Boring characters get killed off as a plot device, so that popular mates can get involved with more interesting people, or simply because fans show a low recognition factor on a network poll. Popular characters "die" because of contract troubles, because they're going to Hollywood, Broadway, etc.

All this is perfectly clear to those involved. For example, the producer of *Search for Tomorrow* notes that heroine Joanne's husband of ten years died "in order to open up more story," and that her next husband would have lasted for ten years if the actor had not decided to go to California. "We were not ready for Tony to die, but Tony died. It was a choice forced on us," she said. Seldom do we find death a choice, even one forced on us. In soap opera, it is understood to be just that—an alternative to moving the character out of town. The writers are in control.

Sometimes the viewers are too. When they get tired of a face, they write in and, if they make a good case, the truck makes its appearance a few weeks later. On the other hand, if viewers object to the killing of a character, they can sometimes rescue him from the jaws of death. Frank Ryan, comatose, was on his way out in the first few weeks of *Ryan's Hope;* however, viewers objected, and Frank is now alive and well with plenty of storyline. It is perhaps the ultimate fantasy; the viewers, ordinary folks, hold the power of life and death over characters with whom they feel involved.

Other psychologically satisfying elements in the soaps may be found in the cast of characters. According to the critics there are stereotypes or archetypes, good and bad people, enjoyable as such. True, these distinctions aren't so gross as they were in radio and early television soaps. Then the good were hopelessly incorruptible and the villains evil incarnate. But still the distinctions are obvious. The audience knows who the bad people are. It waits expectantly for them to do their dirt, and for their eventual punishment or reformation.

It is psychologically satisfying to see situations and people in such unambiguous ways. It is fun to hate a thoroughly bad character, for example. But the soaps provide more than the fun of a morally uncomplicated drama. They pick up on fantasies that are important to women and young girls. In particular they dramatize Oedipal fantasies. In the Oedipal fantasy (also called Electra fantasy) the young girl imagines a blissful existence with a father (father-like character); this is interrupted by a stepmother-like figure, an evil rival who holds the young girl captive—until she is rescued by a young prince who resembles (but is not) father.

Consistent with this general Oedipal outline is the portrayal of men on the soaps. Most of them are father figures, which is to say, doctors or lawyers. In fact, critics have estimated with some disgust that nearly 80 per cent of all men on the soaps are in these two professions. Whereas other romantic stories utilize creative or glamorous types (actors, politicians, artists, tycoons, gamblers and gamekeepers) the soaps prefer as heroes men whose primary quality is stability and family commitment. The hero may be a grand-fatherly confessor (like Dr. Charles Tyler, *All My Children*) or a young idealist (like his grandson Dr. Chuck). He is, in any event, an image of Oedipal longings. From soap portrayals it should be obvious that Doctor is a metaphor for father (and so, to a lesser extent, is lawyer). That Doctor is also the fairy tale equivalent to "prince" is suggested by a number of cases in which a hero is revealed to be a doctor in disguise (David Thornton, *All My Children;* Brad Eliot, *Young and Restless).*

In line with the Oedipal fantasy, there is almost never a bad older man on the soaps (though there are many bad older women). All obvious fatherly types are good; at worse, they are weak or helpless. On the rare occasions when aging male charlatans come along, the audience is surprised. *The Doctors* tried it, compounding the sin of having a villainous older man by making him a doctor as well. The audience, according to the program co-ordinator, was very distressed. Why? "He's an older man," she explained, as if that did explain things. "And also people don't want to believe bad of doctors."

Women in the soaps exist in bad and good archetypes that are also influenced by the Oedipal fantasy. As psychologist Bruno Bettelheim has noted, polarization into good and bad types is an extremely common device in literature, especially in fairy tales. At the Oedipal stage, the polarization of mother-figures allows a child to deal with conflicting feelings. First, the mother is a rival—an "ill-intentioned" older woman keeping her from her father. At the same time, the mother is a caring and loving figure. In other words, the girl sees both a good and bad aspect to her mother. The fairy tale treats them as two different people. This is more satisfying to the girl: through a story like Snow White she can hate the rival stepmother, love the good mother (who exists only in the background) and dream of being rescued one day by the loving and benevolent prince. All aspects of the conflict can be experienced without guilt. As Bettelheim writes, "Thanks to the fairy tale, both oedipal girls and boys can have the best of two worlds: they can fully enjoy oedipal satisfactions in fantasy, and keep good relations with both parents in reality."

So can viewers of the soaps. They can enjoy the polarization that exists in characters like Kate and Phoebe (*All My Children*) or Vanessa and Meg (*Love of Life*). And even when the polarization isn't clearly made, there will usually be an ill-intentioned woman, older or more sophisticated, lurking about to make life miserable for the young heroine (good examples are Linda Patterson Phillips, *Days of Our Lives,* and Margo Flax, formerly, *All My Children*). It's easy to hate her without guilt. Especially since she never gets the doctor/father anyhow.

This is not to say that the soaps are fairy tales, or that audiences are looking for the same kind of gratification as eight-year-olds. Just to cite a couple of obvious points, soaps never have endings at all, let alone happy ones; the polarities of good and bad are much less extreme; and soaps lack the primitive magic and enchantment of fairy tales. However, soaps resemble fairy tales in that their world is peopled with stereotypes from the Oedipal drama; with super-good and bad mother figures; with innocent young heroines; and with all those good but ineffectual fatherly types. Soaps in their images and storyline gratify childhood Oedipal fantasies.

> *The fantasy of the small town (and other nostalgia)*

Another psychologically satisfying polarization in soap opera can be found in the treatment of places—town vs. city. Invariably the bucolic small town is good, and the city bad. This idea is very old and especially American. Thomas Jefferson wrote disparagingly of the city. For our more religious founders, cities were sinful places that fostered prostitution, drinking, crime, gambling and other ills. However true that may be—cities are by nature diverse and chaotic places—it is absurd to hold onto the notion that cities produce only evil things. Yet that notion seems to persist on soaps. The Ryans, through neighborhood life, do manage to retain some virtue in wicked old New York City. But more often soaps imply that people need a small town to really live. It is in the small town that one finds true emotional and moral values. It is there too that one expects to find true relationships. For this reason, even worldly characters return to, and elect to stay in, Oakdale, Rosehill, Pine Valley, etc. Their choice is typically explained to the viewer:

Carol: I've wondered sometimes if you don't get bored living in Oakdale? Living in New York or on the coast must be so much more exciting.

Sandy: Excitement is one thing. Real feelings are another...

—from *As the World Turns*

Trips to the big city are understandably dangerous. Leslie (*Young and Restless*) had the usual bad time of it. During her journey to New York, her purse was stolen, her identity temporarily lost, and she was finally committed to a sanitarium. Rachel (*Another World*) has not fared well either; every time she visits the sophisticated New York art world, her marriage begins to fall apart. Even in the hometown all is not safe from the urban influx. The people are regularly beset by urban villains. Prostitutes, pimps, and carnival performers hail from "Center City." In fact there is hardly a city person who isn't at least a little untrustworthy.

As part of this picture, there's a lingering xenophobia in most soaps—a fantasy that's a constant (and perhaps reassuring) reminder of mother's admonition against talking to strangers. In the small towns (which sometimes resemble extended families if all the illegitimacies and past marriages are counted) strangers, urban or otherwise, have bad intentions. They shouldn't be trusted. Said a character on *Days of Our Lives,* "You can never tell what kind of trouble a stranger can bring into your life." This surely gratifies viewers who need to think that most of life's problems come from outside, rather than inside, their special communities.

The small town simplicity of the soap opera is nostalgic: one might say that it was and always will be nostalgic, because things only seem simple in the past. At any rate, the same nostalgic simplicity is evoked by the social ideas expressed on the soaps. For all the abortions, the miscarriages, the illegitimate births, the tricks of fate, the amnesia victims, the bouts of alcoholism, and other manifestations of domestic mayhem, the message is again countrystore simple. Have faith and hope and family, and you'll find your way. "Faith and prayers work miracles: you believe that, don't you?" says a character in trouble. The audience is clearly meant to believe it. "You have to have faith" is a frequent line, not only in the old inspirational soaps, but in the stylish newer ones. Good grandmotherly types are in the forefront, hoping that the younger people do the "right" thing. And the surprising thing is that there usually is a "right" thing. This is a nostalgia trip indeed.

Ultimately, the soaps provide an old-fashioned antidote to self-assertion, self-actualization, sexual liberation, and other modern therapeutic thought forms. They show that people must suffer, must feel guilt, must experience frustration in love and life goals. But people will go on searching for tomorrow anyhow, with half a chance for happiness. According to the soaps, the way to happiness is family; the solidarity of neighbors and townsfolk; the capacity for occasional personal sacrifices in marriage, parenting, and other moral relationships. And the most old-fashioned thing of all is that it seldom works. The road to happiness seldom leads to that place. There are no euphoric guarantees (as there are on the latest self-assertion or sex manuals). The only thing that can be said is that there's always another chance. "Your future's usually your past, isn't it?" says a 17-year- old prostitute who looks like Alice in Wonderland (*All My Children*). "Not necessarily!" the good doctor says. It turns out that all you have to do is make up your mind and try. It's an old message with a nostalgic feeling. But it is reassuring. For the millions who watch soaps, this simple philosophy is a day-to-day affirmation of hope—and that is surely the most meaningful and powerful satisfaction that an entertainment can provide.

ON AIR

A VIEWER'S GUIDE TO THE SOAPS

4

"Do you watch The Soaps?" is a question we ask in our attempt to gather impressions and information. "No," is the answer, "I just watch *The Young and the Restless,*" or, "No, but I catch a couple of hospital dramas in the late afternoon." Some people really do watch The Soaps—all fourteen of them. Many others watch *a* soap, or two, or three, or a network's worth. They choose their particular soaps for style, content, character, time-slot—whatever is important to *them.* Different soaps for different folks.

Talking about "The Soaps" is about as useful as talking about "the typical viewer." In doing so we necessarily ignore a great many individual differences.

There are, for example, young soaps and old soaps, home-and-family soaps and beautiful people soaps; New York produced soaps and Hollywood soaps; half-hour, hour, and forty-five minute soaps. There are even, some say, sad soaps and happy soaps. Soapland is not the small and homogeneous town so often referred to: it's a mixed neighborhood.

A survey of the soaps shows how and why they differ, and what kinds of audience each attracts.

THE YOUNG AND THE RESTLESS

Perhaps the best place to start is with the soap that is said to have revolutionized daytime TV—*The Young and the Restless.* First aired in 1973, this half-hour CBS show is produced in California (as are *Days of Our Lives* and *General Hospital*). It is a young trendy show, with a Hollywood look. Its storylines are as delightful as adolescent daydreams, and nearly as plausible.

The Young and the Restless is immensely popular. John Conboy (Executive Producer) and Bill Bell (Head Writer) understand the yearning of the audience for something they are not getting elsewhere. It is "unabashed romanticism," says one of Conboy's colleagues. The show is "unabashedly" in support of the hero, the doer—the man who fights against all odds for the woman he loves or the cause he believes in.

More than most soaps, this one makes use of the "Prince Charming" fantasy. Snapper, Brad, Greg and now Lance have arrived on the set in the manner of the man on the white horse. In most soaps the men are respectably handsome. In *The Young and the Restless* they must be sex symbols as well. Shirts are always open to the waist and everyone eligible resembles a nightclub performer. The women too are exceedingly beautiful. Indeed, being a model or beauty queen seems to have been a prerequisite for the job. The show sports a former Miss Teenage America, Miss California, and Miss Phoenix. The young Brooks sisters are all trim as models, with long hair that bounces down the back. Older women (with the exception of poor Liz Foster) have a youthful look and style. Almost everyone looks like a college freshman. Conboy refers to his cast as "beautiful kids," and admits that chemistry is at least part of his criteria in casting.

The message of the show: we can all be young and beautiful. Or: the pleasures and pains of youth (insofar as they are real) belong to you!

Storylines are full of fantasy and fun. The show rests on a Cinderella contrast between the rich Brookses and the poor Fosters (with a true love match between Chris and Snapper). And it exploits other common daydreams. Leslie, a concert pianist who waits for her lover to appear in the front row of a crowded concert hall is typical material; she is next married to a doctor who passes for a newspaper reporter and is secretly going blind. Laurie is an equally glamorous jet set novelist who takes off for Rome and Paris like any beautiful person. There are private yachts, private jets and elegant restaurants reserved for two. Almost everyone can be found in a glamorous setting.

Whole storylines are directed toward adolescent fantasies—those compelling dreams and worries we never really outgrow. We have the boyfriend about to be stolen by a scheming sister (the old Leslie/Brad/Laurie triangle); the fears of meeting a new man (middle-aged Kay Chancellor and Ralph the Plumber, since departed); the need to break away from domineering parents (Brock Reynolds and Kay Chancellor; Lance and Vanessa Prentiss); and over and over again concern with unattractive self-image (most notably in Joann's fight against obesity.)

Throughout, emphasis is on the glamour of life. Problems are often threats to the appearance. Characters are always hiding deformities or flaws. One character, Vanessa Prentiss, goes so far as to wear a veil at all times. Another character, Jennifer Brooks, underwent the soaps' first mastectomy, a seeming violation of her womanly appearance. Even rape is treated as a violation of appearance. "I feel so dirty and disgusting," says Peggy after her rape. "You're *just as beautiful* and innocent as before," says her sister. On *The Young and the Restless* much of what goes on has to do with the maintenance of good sexual exteriors—a problem that emerges for most of us in adolescence. On this show, people do not generally lose their memories, their jobs, their children, or their minds. They lose weight, or virginity, or breasts; and the catastrophic illness in this world of appearances is, of course, the loss of eyesight!

Visually, *The Young and the Restless* is more glamorous than most of the other soaps. There are many, many facial close-ups; actresses often appear in striking white or black gowns, against bright red backgrounds—Hollywood style. They wear dramatic neck scarves, or plunging necklines, or both. And the lighting is extraordinary. "Absolutely I strive for artistic effects," says John Conboy. He claims that it is not unusual for his staff to spend eight or nine hours lighting the sets. The result is a lighting that is generally darker, moodier and murkier than other soaps. Indeed, it is sometimes difficult to make out furniture and other elements of the set. In line with the Hollywood look, bright colors tend to be utilized. The dominant color in makeup and clothing appears to be orange—orangy lipstick, nail polish, scarves.

Music is an integral part of *The Young and the Restless,* as Bill Bell reportedly determined it should be. It is however a case of a little going a long way. The same music is heard time and time again. Although there are themes for particular characters, most music seems to be chosen to fit the situation, and situations do tend to repeat themselves. The theme for the show, which is sexy in a restless, desultory way, has become rather well known. It is sometimes heard in supermarkets (an example of subliminal sell?). And Nadia Comenici used it for her floor exercises at the Olympics. In addition to theme and incidental music, there are performances by actors in character. Practically everyone on the show sings. Beau Kayzer (Brock) plays the guitar, and Janice Lynde (until recently, Leslie) played the piano live for taping.

The look and pace of the show can be (and usually are) described as "restless." One has the sense of constant camera motion, from long shot to close up, from one face to another. Very little time is spent in coffee-table scenes, phone call recaps, or leisurely small talk (the staples of the older soaps). Scenes are short and go straight to the point. One is always being pushed—or jerked—forward.

Recently *The Young and the Restless* cast celebrated its third anniversary. Their accomplishment was something out of the ordinary. Besides being the most influential soap in the television industry, *The Young and the Restless* is usually first in the important 18-40 age group, and is particularly well received on both our trendy coasts.

AS THE WORLD TURNS

The most popular of the old-time serials (and more popular than most of the new and trendy shows) is *As the World Turns*. This CBS show is something of an institution. It has been on the air since 1956, and in the hour format since 1975. It has been called the most old-fashioned of all the soaps, and is the butt of many satires (including Carol Burnett's nightclub act "As the Stomach Turns"). When people poke fun at kitchen scenes and caffeine trips, they might very well be referring to *As the World Turns*.

Fundamentally, *As the World Turns* is a family show about family values. These values are stated and restated by the older characters in the story, particularly by Nancy and Chris Hughes. The show may also be characterized as a doctor-lawyer show. The main families, the Hughes and the Stewarts, are devoted to these two professions. The setting is Oakdale, a typical small town which everyone hates to leave. The population seems to be divided into family people and outsiders who are drifting through, usually as a result of a hurt or disappointment elsewhere.

As the World Turns is concerned with the reactions of people to inevitable suffering. It is concerned with the penalties for caring deeply, and the penalties for letting go. It is also concerned with change, the sometimes painful sloughing off of one's past. About the only reward in sight is family support. The characters get by because someone (usually Nancy Hughes) believes in their future. Half the time she's wrong.

Much of what is offered on *As the World Turns* might be characterized as optimism in the face of the facts. The show is full of comments like "You can't be miserable all the time," "There's a lot to hope for out there," "There's a lot of good things ahead for you," and "You *can* change," (usually said by a family character to an outsider). People who have had

trouble or made trouble frequently announce their intention to "start a whole new life." This philosophizing goes on as characters drop dead, divorce, deceive each other and so forth. Life is not easy, says this soap, but we can get by if we practice those contradictory virtues—acceptance and hope.

In Oakdale, acceptance of life seems to require the renunciation of all fun other than family fun. Single people are a temporary misfortune. A rich bachelor refers to himself as a "well-heeled bum" and says that his kind of life is "not all it's cracked up to be." An attractive single woman who has been around says that "Life has been all fun and games— only the fun really isn't that much fun, and I'm tired of all the games." These characters realize that they must not go looking for personal power or sexual excitement. Stability means absorption into the family structure.

There is little overt sexuality on the show and no attempt to present relevant social issues. "We try to tell human stories that come out of *people*," says John Litvak, Director of Daytime for CBS. The main problems dealt with are infidelity, the management of loneliness and anger, illness (including amnesia) and death. Most evil is the result of weakness— especially selfishness. One actress on the show makes the interesting observation that heroes and heroines are constantly at the mercy of Fate and others (and never have to take responsibility for anything they do) whereas villains seem to take responsibility for everything and everybody. Villains are generally punished in some satisfying way, or, like the famous Lisa (Eileen Fulton), they reform.

Stylistically, the show conforms to most of our old notions of a soap. There are more kitchen sets here than elsewhere. Even Carol Stallings, a young wife who looks like a high school cheerleader, is shown very traditionally in the kitchen. There are many gossip scenes between women and many sit-on-desk routines for men. Although there is very little real action, directors do manage to keep everybody moving during these exchanges. It is said that entire cakes and salads have been prepared in the course of a kitchen scene. And there is reportedly a musical theme that is fondly reserved for those times when Nancy Hughes is kneading dough. The situations are standard, but there is variety in the way they are presented. And, we might add, a certain smoothness.

A dominant tableau on this soap is the woman-with-telephone. If one watches ten minutes, one may see and hear six or seven telephone calls. Much physical action is bypassed in favor of telephone communication. Facial expressions convey the worst of it.

The pace of the show more nearly resembles that of life than drama. The world turns very slowly. Family picnics and holidays are reproduced with dull regularity. People compliment each other's recipes, complain about absent or recently-divorced family members, and sing "Down-by-the-Old-Not-the-New-Mill-Stream." There is a lot of small talk, and excessive recapitulation. "I recapped my whole life once," said John Reilly (until recently, Dan Stewart), "I had an 8½-page monologue and I recapped my *entire life!*" It happens in any number of implausible ways. Marie Masters (Susan Stewart) explains: "Yesterday, I had a big fight scene with Larry (Larry Bryggman, as John Dixon). He comes in and I'm telling him off. In telling him off, I recapped the whole storyline, the past thirteen months." Since characters are constantly telling each other what they did in the past, this is an easy soap to catch on to. And if we miss a few days (months, years) a considerate writer will be sure we know what little has passed in our absence.

Because *As the World Turns* inspires so many satires and put-downs, there is some reason to respond to the question of why it is so popular. Why do eight million people a day watch it? Probably for the same reason they go to family picnics. It's habit; one does care about the people; and it's good to know that somewhere behind us are all those fine family conventions. An unusually high proportion of the audience is in the 55+ age group—a group for whom habit and family continuity are probably important. In addition, there is some evidence that individual characters/actors fulfill a viewer need for inspiration. For example, actresses Kathryn Hays (Kim Dixon) and Rita McLaughlin (Carol Stallings) are, in the story and their personal lives, spiritual models to many. (McLaughlin appears in a popular TV star directory alongside Archbishop Fulton J. Sheen!) The presence of so many good god-fearing doctors is also inspiring. When Dr. Bob Hughes read "Jennifer's Prayer" on the air, so many viewers wrote in to request copies that Procter & Gamble had to hire several people to fulfill the requests.

As the World Turns, over coffee cups, is providing something that is not so readily available in other media. The show is almost always in the top three of the Nielsen's, with highest ratings in the heartland.

ANOTHER WORLD

Another World is an NBC hour-long show, taped in Brooklyn, New York. It premiered in 1964 and went to an hour format in 1975. The show was originally written by Agnes Nixon (creator of *All My Children*). For a long time it was dominated by the Frame and Matthews families, and by the famous Rachel-Steve-Alice triangle. Today *Another World* is not really a home-and-family show. The triangle has been written off. The Head Writer is Harding ("Pete") LeMay. It's a busy, relatively sophisticated show with some of the best dialogue on daytime, and probably the most realistic storylines.

Another World has more characters than most soaps. Although the Frame and Matthews families continue to be important, there are many unattached characters, young people who are not related to anyone. And there are characters from different economic classes. In Bay City, we find rich and beautiful people, with mansions, pools, stables, (and some of the most luxurious sets on daytime); and we find house-servants, poor artists, and hardworking rural types. "I wanted the jet set," says Harding LeMay, "and I also went down one notch below middle class to pick up the Frames off the farm." A sense of class and social mobility is essential to this show. So many of the characters are motivated by a need to get into that other world—the next highest social class (where the people are every bit as troubled).

Another World is, most importantly, a show that pays attention to character and psychology. It does not hint darkly at psychiatric concepts (as does *Days of Our Lives*); instead it deals with ordinary motivations in interpersonal relationships. Oedipal conflicts and all the rest come out in dialogue—not in bizarre and soapy situations.

In the storyline, traditional soap devices are minimized. There is no hospital drama (except incidentally, when someone gets sick and is admitted). There are no amnesia victims, no melodramatic murders or trials. There are also—strange to say—no mysterious illegitimate babies. LeMay's idea of a good twist is to deliver a baby of middle-aged parents (Ada and Gil). Like many situations in *Another World,* this one allows for gentle comedy and poignant relationships between the generations.

The storyline does not rely heavily on Fate. Little happens that cannot be explained by reference to characters' strengths, weaknesses, or backgrounds. Villains (such as Iris or Willis) are understood, and usually forgiven. Good characters too suffer from ordinary flaws (the chief one seems to be jealousy). Far-out things happen here, as on other soaps, but they are more believable. For example, when Beatrice kidnaps granddaughter Sally, her motives are clear every step of the way, and her explanation at the end is not only convincing—it is beautifully moving. Stories do not seem to have been created merely as a means of exciting the viewer; they grow out of characters.

Because the role of Fate is minimized, and people are made to take responsibility for their lives, there is a strong sense of right and wrong in this soap. Characters often discuss the principles on which they act, or the ways in which they have failed one another. People who act on the wrong motives are shown to be unhappy. Over the long-run, characters undergo changes in the moral personality. The most famous example is Rachel (Victoria Wyndham), for many years the evil lady of Bay City; she has been transformed into a lovely woman, with a strong regard for what is right and wrong. Willis seems to be undergoing a similar transformation.

As for the setting, it is generally more cosmopolitan and sophisticated than that of other shows. Characters deal in corporate mergers, architectural contracts, art showings, and other glamorous business beyond the experience of most viewers. There are long business lunches and stylish cocktail parties, as well as the more usual coffee confrontations.

The pace of the show is busy—busy in the manner of a big Bach fugue. Instead of one strong melody or storyline, there are themes in imitation. A scene between older characters will be followed by a complementary scene between young people. Characters seem to be rushing about delivering advice and gossip. ("Would you like to talk about it?" seems to be the most common line.) The show does lack the focus that would be provided by one dominant, heart-rending storyline. But it offers continual stimulation, whether or not one watches every day. One doesn't watch in order to see what will happen, but rather because one enjoys seeing what does happen.

Visually *Another World* is very chic. Most of the wealthy characters are also "beautiful people" with a youngish look. The large cast, and the spread in age and social situation, adds to a visual impression of variety. Clothes and furnishings are chosen with fine attention to detail; there is hardly a scene in which there are not interesting textures and objects in background and foreground.

Another World reaches about seven million households daily. It is the only soap which seems to appeal equally well to across all age groups.

ALL MY CHILDREN

All My Children is a light-hearted soap—perhaps the only light-hearted soap on the air. It may also be characterized as a home-and-family soap, in the doctor-lawyer formula. The setting is the small town of Pine Valley. The major families are the Tylers (who founded the town) and the Martins.

All My Children was created and originally owned by Agnes Nixon, who also wrote or created *Another World* and *One Life to Live*. Today the show is owned by ABC; but Nixon retains creative control and her production company is listed as producer. As of January, 1977, *All My Children* is still in the half-hour format, but there are pressures to move to an hour, and this may well happen in the Spring of 1977.

In its home-and-family orientation, *All My Children* very much resembles traditional soaps. But there are differences in tone. *All My Children* seldom succumbs to dark feelings of loneliness or instability (as does *As the World Turns*) or to sexual despair (as does *Days of Our Lives*). On *All My Children,* there is little serious evil. Bad characters like Phoebe, Erica, Mrs. Lum, or Benny Sago, tend to be fun, or funny. They do not ask much of us. For example, when Phoebe Tyler is left drinking alone on Christmas Eve, she gives a sarcastic, rather maudlin toast. If she pities herself, we don't. On *As the World Turns,* a character in the same predicament would suffer visibly and so would we. Indeed there is remarkably little real suffering on *All My Children,* compared to other soaps—little at least that we must take seriously. Many viewers seem to identify with the writers—speculating on what development will take place next—instead of sympathizing with the troubled characters.

If there is a message to the show, it is that people with all their destructive emotions are "only human"; and that happiness is best found in the sharing of experience with a loved one, within the context of an extended family. Characters tell one another that they can find happiness if they do not demand too much of themselves or others.

The show is, in other words, optimistic. Dialogue is shot through with references to hope and faith. "You have to have faith that things will work out" is said in many forms, and very often. One character will tell another that her problem can be solved. "All I have to hold onto is that hope," is the typical response. Men spend a lot of time encouraging younger women, who are fatalistic, guilt-ridden, irrational, and sometimes right.

It is said that as much as 30% of the audience for *All My Children* is male. Well, there really are an awful lot of very admirable men on this show (Dr. Charles, Dr. Chuck, Dr. Frank Grant, Lincoln Tyler, Danny Kennicott, Paul Martin, etc.,etc.). Except for Phil Brent, who has been troubled, male characters are generally rational or reliable. The only bad guys are people who don't belong in Pine Valley and who do not stay (for example, Hal Short, Benny, and Tyrone the Pimp).

Most of the dramatic interest comes from women. Villains are delightfully overdrawn. Phoebe and Erica are so bad as to be funny, and so good as to set all kinds of improbable plots in motion. The story, however, tends to revolve around sensitive, vulnerable types like Tara, Kitty, Anne, Ruth, and Donna. Here there is an effective mixture of real-life and fantasy-based material. Ruth's marital breakdown was an adult situation, sensitively played (at least until the end). This was, typically, off-balanced by a fantasy of the innocent prostitute (Donna), and the search for the long-lost mother (Kitty). *All My Children* treats difficult life problems, such as the maintenance of marriage and career. But fortunately there are always a few fun-and-far-out storylines going at the same time. Most fun (and more heavily drawn here than elsewhere) are confrontations between black and white, right-and wrong-headed characters (Mona vs. Erica; the good black doctor vs. the bad black pimp).

Although *All My Children* is a modern-looking show, with a young following, it is respectful of old soap conventions. The show features an eternal triangle, complete with a child who does not know his own father (the Phil/Tara/Chuck triangle). Both Chuck and Phil refer to little Phil as "my own son," as Tara stands by beautifully and usually in tears. There are also the usual troubled pregnancies and well-timed illnesses. (Who would have thought that a healthy-looking man like Chuck Tyler would collapse from kidney disease exactly when marriage, then divorce, were imminent; or that Joe Martin would need an emergency appendectomy at the very moment his wife was set to run off with another man?) True, there are some social issues: a speech against war; some rumbling about drugs and women's lib; a not-very-well-integrated sequence on child abuse. But this is essentially a fun romantic drama. We listen to the women's lib rhetoric, and feel good about it, but what we really want to know is whether *she* will stay married to *him*.

All My Children plays more story, at any given time, than most other soaps. Yet it is easy to follow. It's well paced: different storylines move at different tempos, with major stories moving quickly. The lighting is exceptionally bright and clear. Generally recaps are re-presented or re-dramatized, rather than merely stated. Flashbacks-in-the-mind are an important (though perhaps corny) reminder of what has passed before. Music is essentially dramatic, ranging from surrealistic modern sounds (for emotional disturbance), to swarmy violins (for Tara and Phil's theme).

All My Children is usually in the top three of the Nielsen ratings and is especially popular at college campuses and high schools. It has received more than usual press attention, partly because of the publication of Dan Wakefield's *All Her Children* and rather lively public relations campaign that accompanied it.

DAYS OF OUR LIVES

Days of Our Lives is an NBC California show which premiered in 1965 and went to an hour format in 1975. It is the show which begins with a rather lengthy and distraught prologue, followed by a logo which consists of an hour glass, under which the voice of Macdonald Carey is heard to say, "As sands through an hour-glass, so are the days of our lives." The show's Head Writer is Pat Falken-Smith. The twelve month outline or "bible" is provided by Bill Bell, who also writes *The Young and the Restless*. *Days of Our Lives* is known as the most daring of the soaps—given to racy love scenes, interracial romances, artificial insemination, and discussions of frigidity and impotence. It has even shown a young man who believed he was a homosexual (he was soon set right). When bona fide homosexuality finally appears in daytime, it is expected to appear first on *Days of Our Lives*.

The show is not, for all of this, racy. Very little is going on here that isn't going on elsewhere. The characters simply appear more frustrated about it. The show is not licentious; it is horny. Many of the characters suffer from unrequited or unconsummated love. Much of the sexuality is conveyed by conversation, erotic facial posing, and suggestive music.

The content is surprisingly staid. There is an emphasis on formal, sacred arrangements. Marriage, engagement—even living together— continually merit the attention of Grandmother Alice Horton, a warm and tolerant matriarch who is known to be religious. Conventional values are espoused (though not always honored) by the entire Horton family. Run-around women remember romantic tunes from the past, and long for settled family life. This is not altogether a racy soap.

It is, however, a sensuous, darkly romantic soap. It does not seem to be set in the same apple-pie-normal town as, say, *All My Children* or *As the World Turns*. There is little overt optimism. The message seems to be that we are all very deep and driven people; that we can get by only if we learn to accept help (therapy or love) from others. "We all have problems, but if we tackle those problems together, they can be overcome...," says a typical character at a group meeting.

The vocabulary of the show is heavily psychiatric. Characters "space out," have "hang-ups," attempt to get their "heads straight on." They tell each other "stop analyzing me," or "stop playing therapist." One character is told rather bluntly that he goes through therapists "like a kid goes through a box of cracker jacks." It seems a justifiable complaint. This is a show on which the psychiatrist has a breakdown; and even the wise Grandmother Horton is heard to say that she hopes to "get her head together."

Thematic material is consistent with this psychiatric style. Characters endure much stress as a result of secrets from the past (which is thematically equivalent to the unconscious). An unusual number of children do not know who mommy or daddy is. And there is a lot of sexual rivalry and interest between generations. (Julie is endlessly in love with, and now married to, her mother's ex-husband; Trish was pursued by her stepfather, while Mary is attracted to, yet repulsed by, hers.) Love is also a heavy matter. Whereas most soaps have enough trouble simply throwing lovers together, this one must tackle the problems of impotence and frigidity. "Making love is psychological as well as physical," remarks one of show's amateur therapists. And so it is.

Despite the rational overlay of psychiatric concept, *Days of Our Lives* does seem to believe in what we might call sexual determinism: various characters are inexplicably and fatally drawn to each other (and just as inexplicably and fatally attached to someone else). On *Days of Our Lives* we don't find "true love" so much as grand passion. When Robert LeClare of "Doug's Place" sings "The Girl I Love Belongs to Somebody Else" he is singing everybody's theme song, including his own.

Because characters seem to be ruled by inexplicable passions and attachments, motivation is not always obvious. It is not at all clear why people do the very interesting things they do. ("All you can say about these people is that they're awfully mixed up," is one viewer's comment.) The off-and-on romances of Julie and Doug and Amanda and Neil are historical cases in point. It's not clear why the women change their minds—why Amanda would adamantly refuse to marry Neil one moment, then, on his wedding night, leave a message on his answering service reversing her decision (too late, of course). Nor is it clear why Neil would rush into another marriage on a mere refusal from this changeable woman. Over the years, Julie's maneuvers (with every man in town) have been no better motivated, though surely as interesting.

Stylistically, the show is ultra-romantic, West-coast elegance. There is intensity, but not much action. Much is conveyed by position of characters vis-a-vis each other—by romantic tableau, in other words. Lighting is suggestive and moody. Faces are made up (even when a character comes out of brain surgery, she wears eye-shadow). Music tends to be hypnotic, repetitive, though there are occasional bursts of old romantic songs, either in the soundtrack or in the nightclub setting of "Doug's Place." The sound is well controlled for romantic effect. Thunderclaps come at the ends of sentences; and when two characters are talking in "Doug's Place," that Place, though packed, will be quiet as a tomb.

The pace of drama is, according to reviewer Jon-Michael Reed, "a deadly, snail's pace." The stories are "interminably prolonged to incredible proportions." In many scenes, there is a sensuous, sleepwalky tone that is neither unattractive nor inconsistent with the heavy theme of the drama. And virtually everyone has noticed that this soap has some of the genre's most accomplished handwringers. Susan Seaforth Hayes (as Julie) and Bill Hayes (as Doug) are perhaps the most popular couple in daytime TV. They even made the cover of *Time* Magazine. Other stars with vocal fan followings are Patty Weaver (Trish Clayton), Jed Allan (Don Craig), Wesley Eure (Mike Horton, Jr.), Diedre Hall (Marlene Evans), and Tina Andrews (Valerie Grant). The show receives more than a little publicity, and attracts a particularly devoted fan following. It falls in the middle range of soap popularity, with between five and six million households tuning in each day.

RYAN'S HOPE

Ryan's Hope (now almost two years old) is said by those in the television industry to be the most ambitious of the newer soaps. It may also be the happiest soap. The show is written and produced by Claire Labine and Paul Avila Mayer, who formerly wrote for *Love of Life*. Like *All My Children* and *The Young and the Restless*, *Ryan's Hope* attracts a young audience. In fact, when the show first came out, the Nielsen's went up and down, sometimes by as much as 7 points, depending on whether the kids were in or out of school. Part of this appeal may come from the show's newcomer status; this is a soap nobody's parents watched. Equally important is the ambience and attitude conveyed.

As the title suggests, this is supposed to be an optimistic show. Claire Labine likes to say that it is "the opposite of defeatism." There is a belief that characters *can* cope; that the human condition should be celebrated rather than merely endured. The mood is established by the theme music and logo; we see a young version of Mother and "Da" Ryan dance joyfully with an infant son, holding him to heaven at the end.

Ryan's Hope is a home-and-family show and to some extent a doctor-lawyer show. But it differs from others in that it is set in an identifiable place. It's New York City—the place referred to with such horror on the other shows. Since this is New York, and not Oakdale or Rosehill, people of different ethnic backgrounds can be realistically portrayed. The Ryans are not Unspecified Protestants, as are their many counterparts. They are Irish Catholics who frequently refer to their Church, their beliefs, and their traditions. They operate an Irish pub (called "Ryans") in which one has to make excuses for ordering English mustard. Characters from outside the family are also drawn and developed with attention to ethnic background. There are Italian-Americans who call each other "paisano" and attend the Gennaro Social Club. And when an Assistant District Attorney appears, he is identifiably Jewish. Other shows will occasionally throw in an ethnic-sounding name (usually Italian), but *Ryan's Hope* is unique in its use of ethnicity to explain character and behavior.

This is a show in which there is much happy romanticizing about family life. Maeve Ryan is the archetypical mother: warm, supportive, wise, and humorous. "There are some women who can't have too many children," says one character in recognition of her motherly interest in virtually all who set foot in "Ryans." Other members of the family partake of her strength. The Ryans believe in themselves and say so often. Characteristic of the show are two-person scenes in which family trust is exchanged. Upon important occasions, characters say things like, "I want to thank you for a lifetime of love and understanding," or "You're a Ryan and the Ryans are proud of you and are behind you always." Particularly strong are the mother-daughter scenes between Maeve and Mary. (Most of these are written by Claire Labine, who volunteers that she has a very good relationship with her mother.) Characters who do not have families, or are missing a parent, tend to be confused or evil. Everyone understands this. For example, whenever Jack Fenelli so much as frowns, characters begin harping on his lack of family.

In order to put across this romantic sense of family, Labine and Mayer have created a whole mythology of the old Ryans in Ireland, and younger Ryans in childhood. Hardly a day goes by without Mary or Frank relating some long and charming anecdote from childhood—or without Maeve and Johnny describing the wedding party, the potato stews, and the first hard, happy years. Babies and children—mothering and fathering—are shown to be the greatest source of joy. Whole situations (and even arguments) are constructed to reveal the need for family continuity. Some viewers find this soap "preachy," or at least heavy-handed in its family values; others find the Ryans and their familial intensity deeply satisfying.

Storylines are smart, strong, and rather less predictable than those on other soaps. Lost parent fantasies and amnesia are avoided—but divorce, accidents, unplanned pregnancies and unresolvable romantic triangles are always going around. The difference is that here, amidst all the problems, is humor. The Ryans have their troubles, but they also have their fun—rowdy, noisy fun, full of good-natured and bad-natured kidding. Family holiday scenes are staged with a skill that any dramatist would admire; they manage to show a large family enjoying itself, while one or two characters in its midst reach the height of a personal crisis. Love scenes manage to be intimate and playful (something often achieved in life, but seldom, it seems, on the soaps).

How successful *Ryan's Hope* will be is not yet clear. Stars like Nancy Addison (Jill Coleridge), Kate Mulgrew (Mary Ryan), John Gabriel (Seneca Beaulac), and Ilene Kristen (Delia Ryan) have already attracted large fan followings. Nielsen ratings are only a point or two below those of *All My Children,* which now follows *Ryan's Hope* on most line-ups. As Labine and Mayer like to point out, that's higher than the first year ratings for *The Young and the Restless.*

ONE LIFE TO LIVE

One Life to Live is an ABC New York show that has recently gone to forty-five minutes. It is daytime's "show of stars." Erika Slezak, Lee Patterson, Jacquie Courtney, and George Reinholt are members of the cast. These are the stars that inspire fan clubs and win straw polls in the magazines. They are the subjects of numerous stories and stunts. For

example, George Reinholt has stripped for photographers and talked about it. (The picture that appeared in the fan magazine was vague below the waist.) Jacquie Courtney shared with her fans the disagreements that led to her highly publicized departure from *Another World*; and she has provided one of the fan magazines with spreads of photos from her personal album.

On *One Life to Live,* Jacquie and George portray Patricia Kendall and Tony Lord. The two had an affair about ten years ago, after which they went their separate ways (Patricia with child) only to be reunited in the present storyline. Patricia's son Brian is, of course, Tony's son, though he will be the last to know it. Patricia and Tony will not be free to marry when they rediscover that they love each other. (Tony is married to Cathy Craig, a neurotic young woman.) However, the fans love to see this couple, as a couple. Jacquie and George—"they just can't stay away from each other" says a fan magazine, referring to the course of their daytime careers. Before coming to *One Life to Live,* the two portrayed Alice Matthews and Steven Frame on *Another World.* Much of their present popularity derives from that earlier relationship.

Jacquie Courtney, as Alice, came to mean a great deal to the viewers of *Another World.* Her eight-year romance with George Reinholt, as Steve, is perhaps the most celebrated in all of soap history. In fact, when a man recalls with pleasant complaints his wife's old addiction to soap opera—when he says she used to greet him at the door with tears in her eyes—he is probably paying tribute to that old relationship between Jacquie and her fans. What makes Jacquie a star? She is unquestionably beautiful; she's a fine actress; and she had, at least on *Another World,* a role that every woman could identify with. As Patricia Kendall on *One Life to Live,* Jacquie continues to lead the straw polls in the fan magazines (sometimes sharing the honor with Susan Seaforth Hayes). But it's a more mature Jacquie. Not the pretty teenager grown up—but a very womanly, very interesting newspaper reporter.

The appeal of co-star George Reinholt is easy to understand. Until recently, the soaps have had few men who are not Establishment types—father figures, at least in appearance. Reinholt has always looked a little more fiery, more dangerous than your Chuck Tyler or Dan Stewart. He is brawny, rough-faced, and given to tragic expressions. He has had (on both *Another World* and *One Life to Live*) a questionable past and a respectable present—a combination no woman can resist. Unlike most soap heroes, Reinholt doesn't look as if he can be dominated by women. He is known to be very difficult to work with (a fact that accounted for Steve's sudden helicopter crash on *Another World*).

And nobody yet has succeeded in marrying him.

Jacquie and George are relative newcomers to *One Life to Live.* The other superstars on the program have been there for many years, and have very devoted followings. Erika Slezak is undeniably one of the loveliest ladies in daytime. According to her fans, she projects "warmth," in character and in person. Certainly she is kind to viewers who contact her or organize on her behalf. Erika is moreover a very fine actress (she studied at the Royal Academy of Dramatic Art in London). And, as every fan knows, she is the daughter of actor Walter Slezak. Erika plays Vicky Lord Riley, the heroine of the show. Her partner and usually-loving husband is Lee Patterson, another superstar.

Like Erika, Lee Patterson has many fans who are totally committed to *One Life to Live.* Most of these fans are women who find him sexy, even though he hardly ever unbuttons his jacket (in the prevailing young and restless fashion). As Joe Riley, Patterson is attractive mostly because he is ruggedly down-to-earth, protective of those he loves. And because of the chemistry between him and Erika. Erika Slezak and Lee Patterson are a couple the fans love to see together, and now, after many years of difficult storyline, they are.

Although Jacquie and George and Erika and Lee are the primary attractions on *One Life to Live,* a number of younger actors seems to be achieving star status. Among these are Michael Storm (Larry Wolek), and Katherine Glass (Jenny Wolek). Tom Berenger, who played Jenny's true love Tim, was also exceedingly popular before Tim met his untimely death. There are few soaps which so derive their popularity from individual stars.

The appeal of the show, apart from its superstars, is harder to identify, in part because *One Life to Live* has changed so over the past few years. It was at one time thought to be one of the young trendy shows. The Jenny and Tim romance was compared to that of Phil and Tara (*All My Children*). Issues were "relevant." Cathy Craig was known to be a feminist. There were a few ethnics and even a Jewish family (the Siegels). In short, storylines were such as to interest college-aged viewers.

Recently, however, *One Life to Live* has begun to sound more like a traditional soap. Adultery, mysterious parentage, kidnapping of babies, etc., is what is happening now—good storylines in the old mold. There have been frequent changes in storyline direction, and inexplicable (though highly interesting) changes in character, particularly among the evil set. Characters are becoming less realistic, more melodramatic. For the present, "relevant" storylines seem to have disappeared. *Time* Magazine described the show as a "sociologist's delight now giving way to careless love...."

One Life to Live is a soap of middling popularity. It reaches about six million households every afternoon. The presence of so many daytime superstars guarantees that it reaches some of soap opera's most ardent, and most organized, fans.

LOVE OF LIFE

Love of Life is a CBS New York show that runs for 25 minutes (the last five minutes of the half-hour are given over to morning or midday news). This is the first soap in the day's line-up; it airs at 11:30 in New York, and as early as 9:30 in the midwest. It is one of the older soaps, having been on the air for some 25 years.

Love of Life is a morally colored drama which began in the contrast between a good and evil sister (Vanessa and Meg) and which continues to show that good triumphs over evil. It is not, however, a simplistic tale. Though bad people suffer, they also bleed. It is pointed out that mothers love their bad daughters as fiercely as their good, and that young adults can and should forgive their parents' failings, etc.

Love of Life was fairly stodgy (and pretty much in trouble) before the fall of 1973. At that point, new writers were hired (Labine and Mayer, now the writers/creators of *Ryan's Hope*). The storyline became more exciting, the pace quickened, and the ratings improved. Characters became younger; no longer could it be said that the youngest character with a storyline was 32 years old! Today the show features an array of characters that seems designed to meet identity and fantasy needs. There is the older meddlesome Meg (the original bad sister); her young

innocent daughter (Cal) and bigamous son (Ben), and their various unsuitable partners. There is the sterling married couple (the Sterlings) and a first rate charmer-villain (Ray Slater). There are, moreover, storylines involving some relevant issues—political corruption, prison reform, teenage alcoholism—all fully integrated into the story.

Storytelling is usually honest. Thrusts of fate may be dramatic or bizarre, but they seem to grow out of character and situation. At any given time, there will be two or three storylines, never more than four. It's an easy show to follow.

It is also one of the more extravagant shows. It seems that *Love of Life* periodically finds itself under budget, and makes up for this by doing expensive on-location shootings. Designers have also gone all-out for some sets—the "Beaver Ridge" restaurant and Piano Bar, for example. Until recently, *Love of Life* kept a $30,000 Jaguar in the basement of CBS studios, and there is still a shameless round bed belonging to Arlene Lovett, the smoldering beauty of the show.

Love of Life is a solid soap of middling popularity—but with a good showing among new viewers (a bit surprising for an older show). On many line-ups, it leads into *The Young and the Restless*.

GUIDING LIGHT

Guiding Light is a New York show in the half-hour format. It is the only soap to have played on both radio and television (identical scripts were aired on the two media from 1952 to 1956). Since 1956, *Guiding Light* has been on television only.

Guiding Light follows in the traditional mold of *As the World Turns*. In fact, it follows *As the World Turns* on most television line-ups. Like *As the World Turns*, *Guiding Light* used to be somewhat inspirational in tone. The original television logo showed a lighthouse with a beacon (guiding light). Things have changed. The current logo is a piece of spare footage someone discovered in the storage bin; it appears as an abstract design under which lights twinkle and modern music plays.

The cast of *Guiding Light* is slightly older than that of, say, *The Young and the Restless*, or *Ryan's Hope*. Characters are mostly Establishment types, doctors and lawyers. About a year ago, *Guiding Light* did introduce two good-looking young men in the modern mold (one was even a singer); but these characters did not fit in, and were subsequently dropped. Recently *Guiding Light* again added younger characters, including two anti-establishment types (Ben and Jim McFarren) and a down-home family (the Stapletons).

Guiding Light used to revolve around the Bauers, just as *As the World Turns* revolves around the Hughes and Stewarts. But when Papa Bauer died, and Bill Bauer was killed off, neither the characters nor writers seemed to know where to turn. Today, the family focus is not so clear. Some continuity is provided by the character of Bert (Mama) Bauer, played for thirty years by half-namesake Charita Bauer. Once a catty, villainous sort, Bert now presides over *Guiding Light* with

matriarchal fervor. As in other traditional soaps, the hospital is a major setting, pregnancy and paternity are real dilemmas, and sudden death is common as a means of solving story problems. There is little real evil—just temporary lapses and much trouble between parents and children. There is perhaps less Momism here than on most soaps. Fathers like Mike Bauer and Ed Bauer have important emotional roles. (Don't ask about their biological roles.)

There are some significant ways in which *Guiding Light* differs from the archetypical old soap. The look is modern. And it's not too kitcheny; Producer Allen Potter enjoys doing on-location shootings, and has tried to be original with settings. The music is more adventurous than on most other soaps. Composer Charles Paul, who writes or has written for *As the World Turns*, *Love of Life*, *All My Children*, *Somerset* and *Guiding Light*, says that it is *Guiding Light* in which he is "given his head." One may hear interesting discordant music where appropriate (under a heart attack, for example). And the relationship of music to text is generally more original or arty than on other soaps.

As an older show, *Guiding Light* has built a loyal following from all age groups, but is particularly strong in the 55+ age group.

SEARCH FOR TOMORROW

Search for Tomorrow is a CBS New York show in the half-hour format. At 25-years of age, it's the oldest show on television, and must therefore be counted as a huge success. It has evolved through the years, and kept up with the times chiefly through the vision of one woman—Mary Stuart. Since the beginning of the show Miss Stuart has played Joanne Vincente (Filmclips of Miss Stuart's initial performance were recently shown at the 25th anniversary party). Miss Stuart, if not exactly sole heroine, is certainly the leading lady of *Search for Tomorrow*. She is joined these days by a whole generation of young people, brought on to meet the needs and explore the problems of the new soap generation. Among these new characters are Liza and Steve Kaslo, Amy and Bruce Carson, and Kathy and Scott Phillips. Favorites in the older generation are Elly and Stu Bergman (who function rather like matriarch and patriarch), and John Wyatt, played by one of

daytime's star personalities, Val Dufour.

Search for Tomorrow is concerned with character development. Certainly there has been time for this. For the last 25 years, according to producer Mary Ellis, writers have been making Jo Vincente more human, more vulnerable. In the early years she was a model, an ideal and unbelievable woman. As the years went by, she was allowed to make mistakes, to be less than perfect in her relationship with others. *Search for Tomorrow* has shown in Jo that having a character on the show for many, many years, is not necessarily restrictive. And that even a very good woman can, with some bad luck, have any number of romances.

Storylines on *Search for Tomorrow* are traditional soap. (Or, given the show's longevity, one might say that storylines on the other soaps are traditional *Search for Tomorrow*.) Serious attention is given to the quality of human relationships, particularly between the four generations on the show. There is much hospital drama—almost as much as one finds on a doctor-lawyer soap like *As the World Turns*. There is perhaps an unusually high incident of murder, attack, and threatened attack. And there are extraordinary weddings. Recent ceremonies for Elly and Stu Bergman and Liza and Steve Kaslo used original texts; thousands of viewers wrote in for copies.

The show does not appear to be committed to presenting relevant issues. Still it does show contemporary problems in relationships, among them the redefinition of male and female roles. Recently, conflicts have developed between Steve and Liza as a result of Liza's unexpected opportunity to become a top fashion model. And, years ago, the first abortion on daytime was undergone by Kathy Phillips, a married career woman who appears to be the only woman on the soaps to have made the conscious choice not to have children. It took *Search for Tomorrow* a long time—six or seven years—to make Kathy a sympathetic character. Even today, viewers who accept her decision are quick to point out that she has, after all, shown maternal affection for Eric, her husband's foster son.

Search for Tomorrow is a popular show among both young and older viewers. In New York, it competes very well against *All My Children,* a show that receives more fashionable publicity. Highly successful in its own terms, *Search for Tomorrow* continues, like its title, to look forward. "Almost everyone on the show has children. And that perpetuates the story," says the producer.

THE EDGE OF NIGHT

The Edge of Night is soap opera's only crime/mystery melodrama. The logo is an outdated, and therefore unrecognizable, shot of Cincinnati (where Procter & Gamble is located). The setting is a city ("Monticello") with a criminal underground and some ethnic diversity. Characters are the standard folk of crime drama; lawyers, police officers, court psychiatrists, upper- and underworld forces.

The show premiered in 1956, and is thus one of the older soaps. It was originally on at dusk (the "edge of night") and was for some years quite popular with men. When it was switched to early afternoon, writer Henry Slesar softened the crime angle and down went the ratings. In 1975, P & G, owner of the show, switched it from CBS to ABC, and the ratings improved. *The Edge of Night* is once more aired late in the day (in New York, it's on at 4:00). Today, the show combines the crime/mystery content with domestic hassles, love triangles (Nicole/Adam/Brandy), amnesiac wanderings, and all the standard happenings of daytime drama.

The main characters of *The Edge of Night* are Adam Drake and Mike Karr, lawyers and crusaders against the underworld. The main problem is that people are being forced into crime by one means or another. Beneath the surface are threats of blackmail, robbery. extortion, arson—and worse. Last year, for example, there were three murders and two attempted murders. There is always one courtroom drama a year, and sometimes two.

"Good" and "bad" characters are perhaps more distinctly drawn on this show than elsewhere. There are real villains, usually short term (for example, Tony Saxon, Clay Jordan). The good characters are not perfect, however. Johnny Dallas, one of the heroes, is a reformed tough from the lower classes and sometimes it shows. Other sympathetic characters (for example, Tracy Micelli, Kevin Jamison) also make mistakes and get into trouble. But they remain heroes of the drama nonetheless. One thing that these characters do better than most is to kid around. There are comic exchanges between Johnny Dallas and Danny Micelli, and an occasional slapstick touch on the part of other characters. There is also more physical action here than on most other soaps: catastrophes such as accidents, fires, and murders are shown rather than merely discussed.

Though many of the problems arise from crime, corruption, investigation, etc., the show is not interested in social problems, *per se*. It is just good daytime drama in which the heroes fight not only on the side of true love and family solidarity, but on the side of law as well.

The Edge of Night is not one of the most popular shows, but it has a devoted following. Rumors are that the show is going through a period of transition.

GENERAL HOSPITAL

General Hospital and *The Doctors* are usually grouped together as daytime's two "hospital soaps." They are similar in format, and have, at different times, been written by the same writers. One actor, Gerald Gordon, has starred on both. However, the shows do differ. And though both have medical titles, they do not have more medical drama, over a period of time, than do shows like *All My Children* or *As the World Turns.*

General Hospital is an ABC California show that has tried to imitate the popular elements of *The Young and the Restless.* It premiered in 1963 (on April 1, the very same April Fools'Day that saw the premier of *The Doctors*). Since that time, the show has gone through many writers, and consequently many transitions. In a soap, "transition" usually translates "slaughter," as each writing team kills kills off the creations of its predecessors. The Hollands, a husband-and-wife team now in control, wrote off a large part of the cast they inherited, with the result that only four or five major characters survive. One suspects that this soap does not fulfill the need for long-term vicarious friendship, and that it is not popular in old age homes.

Characters who have stayed to provide minimal continuity include Dr. Steve Hardy, patriarch of *General Hospital,* and Nurse Jessie Brewer, matriarch. These two middle-aged characters preside over a hospital, not a family. Most of the dramatic interest centers on Leslie Faulkner, a sexy lady doctor who has been distracted from her career first by a search for a long lost illegitimate daughter (now found, now lost) and secondly by a villainous husband (now dead). Most viewers are attracted to Leslie (Denise Alexander). However, Leslie, in her gulli bility and naivete, behaves more like the troubled radio soap heroine than the modern professional woman; her actions are so incredible that viewers, remaining fond, lose patience with her.

The story is full of conventional soap elements. There are murder trials, reported (but not actual) deaths, switched babies, and many, many illnesses. There is also some attention to psychological concepts. Dr. Peter Taylor, psychiatrist and friend to all, conducts one-to-one therapy sessions on the air. In one episode, he persuaded a potential suicide to come off the window ledge. In another, he gave sensible advice to a paranoid who feared his food was being poisoned ("Eat a balanced diet"). There are relevant references to psychosomatic illnesses, neurosis (in women) and sexual inadequacies, etc.

General Hospital is neither so popular as the young and trendy shows, nor so well received as the older traditional ones. It has recently been expanded to a 45-minute format (back to back with *One Life to Live*), and this is expected to help both shows improve on their decent, but not particularly exciting, ratings.

THE DOCTORS

The Doctors is an NBC New York show in the half-hour format. It is, according to the announcer, a show "dedicated to the brotherhood of healing." Like *General Hospital, The Doctors* has gone through many transitions in the last few years. Families that have endured the inevitable purges are the Aldriches and the Powers. Dr. Matt Power is the patriarch of the show, head of hospital and family. None of his positions is secure.

The Doctors is a traditional soap which bases much of its story on marital conflict, love triangles, blackmail, amnesia, etc. It has also treated the topical problem of euthanasia, through the dilemma of a young girl connected to a respirator without any chance of recovery to normal life. (The legal language here was quite close to that in the recent Quinlan case.)

This past year, *The Doctors* began to move away from its core storyline of Matt and Maggie. There's been more sex, more drugs, and many complaining letters. The audience is older, and "very staid and very righteous," according to one of the program's decision-makers. They can accept kissing, but not bed scenes—not even between their favorite characters.

The show does other interesting things. On *The Doctors*, we have the first doctor in soapland who operates unnecessarily. (We've suspected many others.) There is also a story developing around the problems of male menopause.

At present, *The Doctors* seems to be in one of its transitional periods. The direction of the storyline is unclear—and so is the future of the show. There are rumors that *The Doctors* will be cancelled, and if so this will happen in the spring. However, the ratings for the show are nowhere near as low as those of the recently cancelled *Somerset*, and it may well survive.

LOVERS AND FRIENDS

The newest soap opera, *Lovers and Friends,* premiered on January 3, 1977. It is an NBC half-hour show taped in Brooklyn, in studios adjacent to those which house *Another World.* The Executive Producer and Head Writer, Paul Rauch and Harding LeMay respectively, are from *Another World.* Clearly NBC hopes that *Lovers and Friends* will be as popular as *Another World* for some of the same reasons. (An earlier spin-off of *Another World, Somerset,* was not successful.)

Lovers and Friends is set in an identifiable location—a wealthy suburb of Chicago. (It is perhaps interesting that the two newest soaps, *Lovers and Friends* and *Ryan's Hope,* are the only soaps to be set in real places.) The action centers around the Cushing and Saxton families. As in *Another World,* generation conflicts are to be very important. So are class and wealth difference. It appears that the show will be concerned at some level with the negative aspects of social mobility.

Lovers and Friends is billed as a bold new soap about the way love is today. Naturally, it has a healthy number of bold young characters (ranging in age from fifteen to twenty-eight). People in the younger generation have names like Bently, Megan, Austin, Desmond, and, yes, even Rhett. Given LeMay's interest in life stages and generations, it is unlikely that the action will be dominated by young people, or even by older people with youngish figures and problems (as is the case in *The Young and the Restless*). However, the first strong storyline concerns a love triangle involving a Cushing daughter and two of the "Saxton boys." Since the Saxtons are not so classy as the Cushings, it is not certain that either of the brothers will luck out. It promises to be a storyline of young love and parental prejudice.

IMAGES OF STYLE

5

At one time, soap opera scripts contained flattering references to household products. On radio, it was not unusual for the heroine to interrupt her dramatic speculations with a reference to Bab-O cleanser—which is exactly what happens on *Mary Hartman, Mary Hartman* today. There is, says spoofy Mary Hartman, no great difference between the images we find on soap commercials and on soap opera itself. She's right. The soaps sell a lot more than soap, detergent, laundry additives, furniture polish and oven cleaners. They sell a vision of American life. They dictate styles and fashion to a degree unsuspected by almost everyone.

For example, the soaps sell clothes. One noted American designer admits that women relate more to the soaps than to *Vogue* or *Harper's Bazaar*. When she stages fashion shows in Wichita or St. Louis, she is always approached by viewers who want to buy the dress that Susan Stewart wore last week. It's the next best thing to having your clothes on a celebrity—say, Jacqueline Onassis. Natalie Walker, Costume Designer for *As the World Turns* (a show that gives designers both audio and visual credit) reports that hundreds of calls are received from women who want to buy the latest costumes from Cinnamon Wear, Nipon, Ted Lapidus, Calvin Klein, Valentino and other designers featured on the show. While *Vogue* reaches 2 million households a month, Miss Walker reaches between 7 and 8 million households *every weekday*.

Household props and furnishings interest viewers almost as much as clothes. *Another World,* a show with extraordinary home and office sets, regularly receives letters from viewers inquiring where they can buy the curio in Iris' livingroom, or requesting that Ada's kitchen draperies be changed.

Both viewers and producers are aware of status implications in these images. "There's a difference between producing poor and producing rich," says Executive Producer John Conboy (*Young and Restless*). He explains: the poor Foster's home has "a clean look, without frills, sparsely decorated." The well-to-do Brooks' home is elegant, "understated," with doors and leaded windows from a nearby Pasadena mansion. Every care is taken to point up the contrast. Should the same coffee pot appear in the poor and rich homes (as happened on one soap, now defunct), there will be protesting letters.

Viewers look to the soaps not only for story; not only to find out how to get clothes white and bright. They look for fashion and style images. To see what kind of sportswear is being worn, at what length, by the best women. To see the nightclubs, patios, and livingrooms of daytime's very rich.

The Coleridge girls are the image of well-to-do good taste on *Ryan's Hope*. Here Jill Coleridge models a lounging gown.

Fashion images

As the World Turns likes the classic idea, translated into contemporary fashion, as on Susan Stewart (left). The tie-less look on Dan Stewart is somewhat unusual for the show. Bob Hughes (bottom center) is more typical Oakdale. High(er) fashion looks can be found on Erica Brent (*All My Children*) who used to be a model (right and far right), and on Leslie Eliot (*Young and Restless*) who appears in a modish peasant dress (top center).

The braless look seen on *The Young and the Restless* is not yet acceptable on *As the World Turns* or *Another World.* Julie's classy evening look, with décolleté, is seen on *Days of Our Lives* (right). Since Julie's married, though, she tends to spend more time in blue jeans and other informal clothes—and fans suspect a change in image.

In the wardrobe room

Costume Designer Natalie Walker (upper right) selects "good solid American design" for *As the World Turns*. Character Anne Jeffers (right) returns today's costume to the wardrobe rack at *Guiding Light*. In the wardrobe room of *Another World,* Iris, the show's wealthiest character adjusts her hat (left). According to Lewis Brown, Costume Designer, both the character and the actress (Beverlee McKinsey) have a canny sense of "what works." Iris seldom wears the same garment twice. Also on *Another World,* Sharlene Matthews (lower left) has a younger, more middle class look. She and Russ Matthews are assisted by the wardrobe mistress. Women's clothes for the show come mainly from Bonwit Teller. Mr. Brown personally shops for about 40 characters, and it's not unheard of for him to spend $10,000 in one morning at a summer sale.

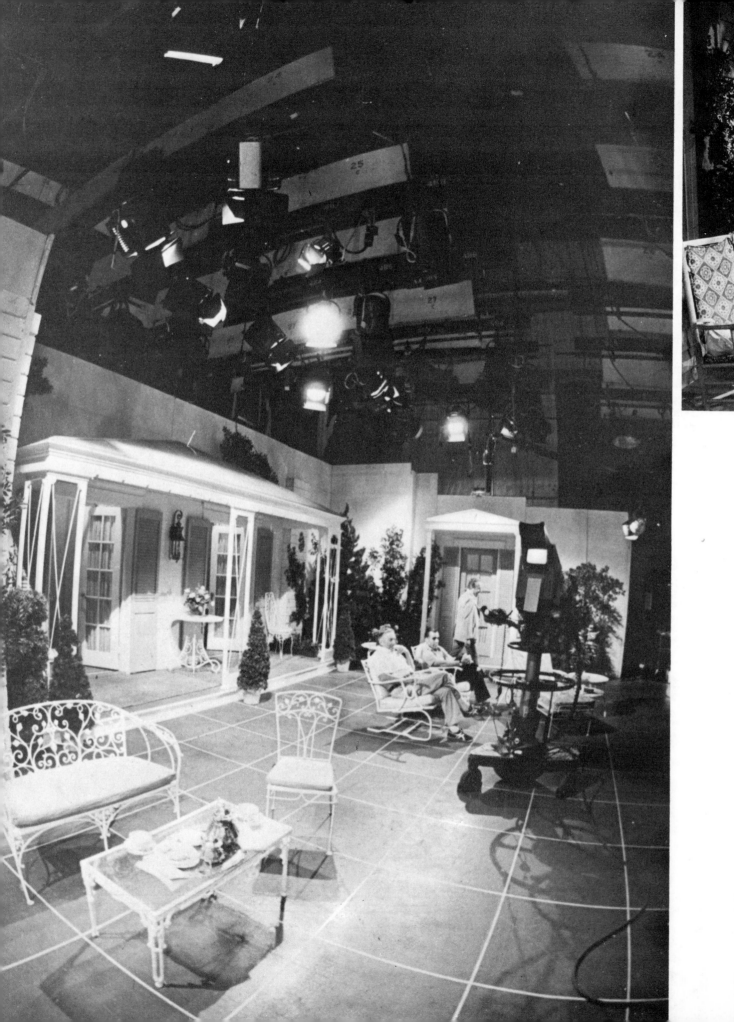

Class cliche̍s reflected

Much social information is conveyed in set design. Above, *All My Children* puts across the "small town suburban look," as Danny Kennicott and Tara chat on Grandmother Martin's porch. At left, Iris's patio shows us how the rich take the summertime; the full picture, including pool, can be seen in the floor plan of the set designed by Otis Riggs, Art Director (*Another World*). The kitchen set also varies in style. Above right, is the simple middle class kitchen of Mary Ellison (*As the World Turns*). Below right, is the institutional kitchen behind "Ryans"; as usual there is more drama than cooking. The confrontation here is between Maeve Ryan and Jill Coleridge (*Ryan's Hope*).

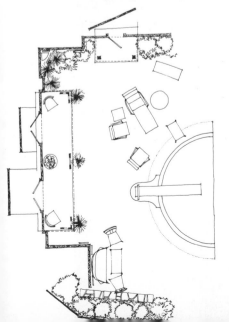

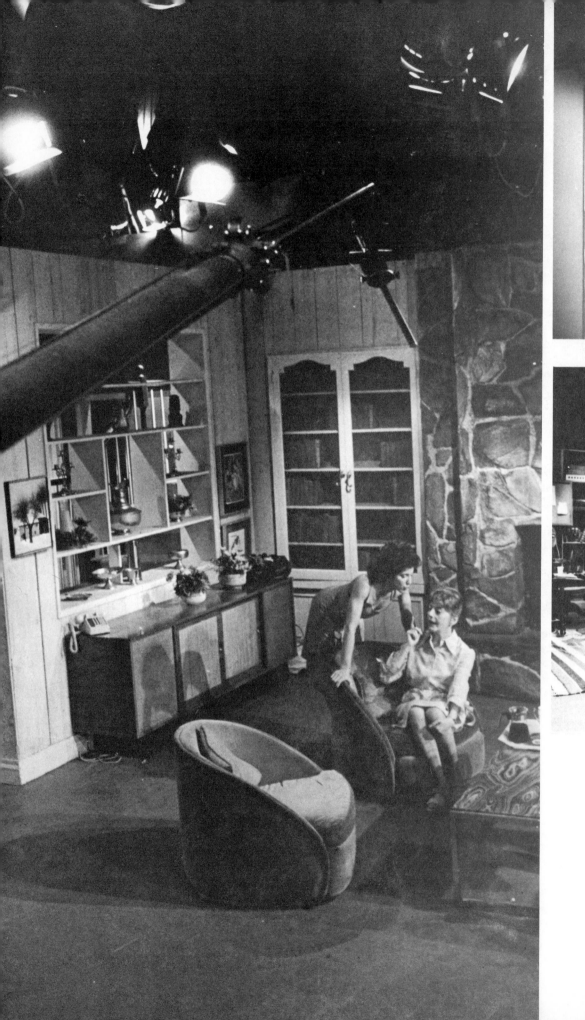

Domestic styles

Livingroom and bedroom sets are designed to reflect the characters who inhabit them. At left, Alice's country house has a spacious upper middle class look (*Another World*). Iris's livingroom (top center and left) has a "sophisticated French feeling," with French-shaped windows and fireplace, and an overall feminine tone (*Another World*). Very different is the urban studio apartment of Mary and Jack, a young married couple on *Ryan's Hope* (left). And standard soap is the contemporary livingroom of Eleanor Conrad (*The Doctors*); the tufted sofa (right) appears in many shows and settings. Extravagent decor is usually the mark of an unsympathetic character. Wouldn't you know that Arlene and Ben in the round bed (below) were wrongly and secretly married (*Love of Life*)?

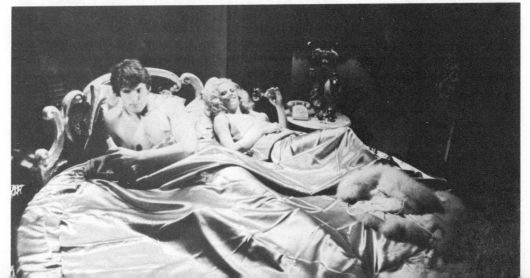

Restaurants and bars

The restaurant is an important meeting place on most soap operas. It's also a showpiece. "Ryans" (upper right) is authentic Irish and intentionally tacky. It's the only working bar on daytime, so who cares? Below right, the Piano Bar at "Beaver Ridge" is *Love of Life's* conception of the kind of spot most viewers would reserve for that special occasion. The whole Beaver Ridge set, including Rick Latimer's behind-the-bar office (above left) reportedly cost about $30,000. A restaurant with more casual decor appears on *Days of Our Lives* (below left). Doug's Place is the frequent scene of intimate conversations.

ARCHETYPES

There must have been a time in soap opera history when characters were well-defined types; when heroes were heroes, villains were villains, and almost nobody was in-between. There must have been such a time—because critics of soap opera and hosts of talk shows on the subject always allude to it. They describe, with some presumption, a standard cast of characters which is interchangeable from show to show.

If ever this was the case, it's not today. Soap opera characters are seldom merely Good or Bad. Though some male characters are superficial, females almost never are. Most display the depth, contradictions and growth that we associate with human behavior. The heroines have their share of weaknesses—not only for love, but for alcohol or crime, for example. Villains are not what they used to be either. Shows like *Another World, Ryan's Hope* and *Love of Life* take great care to present a full psychological picture; even the villain of the moment is perceived as an individual with "needs."

If there has been a general change in soap opera thinking, it can be seen rather clearly in the career of Meg Hart (*Love of Life*). Meg Hart was on the show for its first ten years. She was played unabashedly, unrelentingly "black." She had not one redeeming quality. Eventually viewers (and writers) tired of her and sent her packing. When she was brought back to Rosehill some eight years later, she was altered, deepened, by her life off screen. Now, says Associate Producer Tom de Villiers, "we play her with feeling; she bleeds. She doesn't always like the things she does...she has dimension."

Another example can be seen on *Another World,* in the character of Rachel. For many years Rachel was an arch-villain of a highly enjoyable variety. Gradually she began to be perceived as a woman of greater dimension. Writer Harding LeMay says that he inherited an "utterly worthless girl" and subtly transformed her into "a girl who had certain drives and needs and was very dissatisfied with life; and then once those needs were fulfilled; once she'd married the richest man in town...a man old enough to be the father who had walked out on her, she became a different kind of person." An entirely understandable process. Other characters (for example Ann Larimer, *The Doctors*) have undergone the reverse transformation. Originally a heroine of sorts, Ann has become an embittered and unsympathetic character, as a result of romantic misfortune. Characters like Ann and Rachel function not as types, but as individuals.

This is not to say that we may make no generalizations or construct no stereotypes around the soap opera character. It is only to say that we can do so no more in daytime drama than in any other kind of drama. There are certain archetypical characters in the soaps, but they are characters of depth and individuality. Young actors and actresses commonly say that they represent some of the most "challenging" roles available. If we look at the archetypical roles, and the variations from show to show, we can see why this is so.

1

2

3

The young-and-vulnerable

1. Liza Walton Kaslo (*Search for Tomorrow*)
2. Cal Aleata Latimer (*Love of Life*)
3. Kitty Carpenter (*All My Children*)
4. Peggy Brooks (*Young and Restless*)
5. Trish Clayton (*Days of Our Lives*)
6. Hope Bauer (*Guiding Light*)
7. Leslie Brooks (*Young and Restless*)
8. Tara Tyler (*All My Children*)

romantic heroine

Probably the most appealing of all soap opera types is the young romantic heroine. The role may be played as the wholesome ingenue (Hope Bauer) or the chaste and trusting young wife (Carol Stallings, Liza Kaslo). Or it may be played as an insecure woman with a romatically troubled past (Kitty Carpenter, Sharlene Matthews). It is, however, almost always played by a slender person with long hair. And it's an emotional role: our heroine is strong in her feelings and indecisive in her actions—which means that she is "torn." In this weakened emotional state, she is prime target for villainous plots and cruel Fate. These are good girls who trust too easily and fall too hard. The viewer sees it coming—and that's where the handwringing comes in (it's not all done on screen).

1. Willis Frame (*Another World*)
2. Dorian Cramer Lord (*One Life to Live*)
3. Cameron Faulkner (*General Hospital*)
   - recently killed
4. Paul Summers (*The Doctors*)
5. Ray Slater (*Love of Live*)
6. Roger Coleridge (*Ryan's Hope*)
7. Tyrone (*All My Children*)
8. John Dixon (*As the World Turns*)
9. Jay Stallings (*As the World Turns*)

The old-fashioned villain

5

6

As Hamlet long ago discovered, practically anyone can be, or turn out to be, a villain. However, not everyone can be the kind of villain we love to hate. That distinction belongs to what is sometimes called the old-fashioned villain, or "totally black character." (It seems that there are so few black characters in the usual sense of the word that "black" can still be understood to mean "villain!") What is delightful about the totally black character is that we do not need to feel sorry for him; he's just *too* bad. He allows us the pleasure of hating without the usual penalties of guilt. What do such characters do to warrant such response? They intentionally hurt people; they set in motion evil and preposterous plots; they play upon the vulnerable with lies and blackmail. And they show themselves to be guilty of the soap's Unpardonable Sin, which is pure and premeditated selfishness. Though some soaps take pains to explain the villain, and others go so far as to rehabilitate him, in most cases the character is discredited and ostracized. The old-fashioned villain remains one of the more popular of soap opera characters. But he is a disappearing type. In fact, we've only been able to find five who really meet the test. Others are in a fair way of establishing *some* viewer sympathy, because they've been punished for their black deeds (John Dixon, Jay Stallings), or because they did it all for love (Roger Coleridge).

8

7

9

...and runners-up

Some women are always in devious pursuit of a man who doesn't—and shouldn't—belong to them. In love, they are the natural rivals of the good characters. Too often they create misunderstandings and misfortune for purely selfish reasons; too often they oppose the true love relationship we wish to see fulfilled. Generally the Rival is a woman who is not completely comfortable with her environment or its prevailing values. She is on the move; she is money- and status-conscious; she's dangerous for now but sure to be unhappy in the end. Because the storyline allows her to pursue one man after another, she may also be perceived as sexually aggressive. Examples range from overdrawn neurotic types like Iris Carrington and Erica Brent, to threatening but otherwise sympathetic types like Valerie Conway. The Rival is sometimes referred to as Bitch-Goddess—because that's how we tend to see our rivals, isn't it? She is invariably beautiful, with clothes to match.

1. Jennifer Pace (*Search for Tomorrow*)
2. Erica Brent (*All My Children*)
3. Olive Gordon (*Another World*)
4. Valerie Conway (*As the World Turns*)
5. Iris Carrington (*Another World*)

The rival

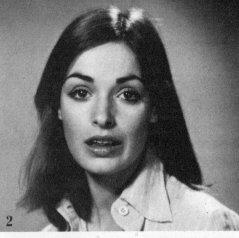

The suffering antagonist

Not quite villains, these ladies may be properly called antagonists. They create trouble for our favorite characters, and very often display selfishness, jealousy, and other unattractive traits. Nonetheless, they are among the most popular and durable soap opera characters. Like us, they have needs and weaknesses; like our friends, they provoke complicated emotional responses, ranging from momentary annoyance to deepest empathy. These are people who make mistakes and seem to pay for them. We can't afford to identify with them *all* the time.

1. Delia Reid Ryan (*Ryan's Hope*)
2. Brooke Hamilton (*Days of Our Lives*)
3. Vicki Paisley (*Somerset*)
4. Susan Stewart (*As the World Turns*)
5. Cathy Craig Lord (*One Life to Live*)
6. Stacy Wells (*The Doctors*)

Mr.Right

Believe it or not, soap opera characters allude now and then to "Mr. Right" (or more delicately, to "the Right Man"). To soap heroines, Mr. Right resembles the man invariably recommended by one's parents and grandparents: good family, good manners, good job, and three-piece Brooks Brothers suit. This is no place for quirky romantic heroes with their uncertain tempers. Mr. Right is a doctor, lawyer, or newspaper magnate. He is tall, slender, attractive, and maybe even sexy. But his appeal is his stability. He is professionally and financially secure; and he likes nothing better than to spend time with deserving members of his family. The soaps may play out fantasies and day-dreams, but in male-female relationships, they don't cater to adolescent tastes. The dark, brutal-but-gentle stranger has been outclassed by the boy next door (fine young man, they call him).

1. Mike Bauer (*Guiding Light*)
2. *Lincoln Tyler (*All My Children*)
3. *Tony Lord (*One Life to Live*)
4. Bob Hughes (*As the World Turns*)
5. Gary Walton (*Search for Tomorrow*)
6. Dan Stewart (*As the World Turns*)
7. Julian Cannell (*Somerset*)
8. *Frank Ryan (*Ryan's Hope*)

*These characters are currently married, but that doesn't alter their Mr. Right status. Mr. Right tends to marry women who are Wrong for Him, or who are doomed by Fate. And soon he's in the running again.

4

7

8

1. Lance Prentiss (*Young and Restless*)
2. Doug Williams (*Days of Our Lives*)
3. Kevin Thompson (*As the World Turns*)
4. Rick Latimer (*Love of Life*)
5. Nick Davis (*All My Children*)

The soaps recognize that Mr. Right (or *Dr*. Right) is a mature fantasy, and that many viewers retain the adolescent taste for the questionable or disreputable lover. This is the man of darker passions—the man we hate to love, but do. He doesn't exist in the soaps. But he almost does: we do have the Former Playboy, the slightly mysterious and not altogether stodgy man who is, as they say, "attractive to women." By the time this character appears on daytime, he has forsaken his playboy existence, and sought love in the arms of a favorable woman (or two). About the only sign of his previous existence is his money (since he's not a doctor or lawyer, the money is probably a bad sign!). A classic instance of the type is the now-deceased Steven Frame, who first appeared on *Another World* as a well-heeled bachelor of uncertain background. Steve never quite deserved the romantic attentions of lovely Alice Matthews, or the 9 million women who followed him daily. But he got it.

The former playboy

The meddlesome and villainous mother/grandmother

1. Geraldine Whitney (*Edge of Night*)
2. Liz Matthews (*Another World*)
3. Meg Hart (*Love of Life*)
4. Phoebe Tyler (*All My Children*)

As children we sometimes fantasize about the villainous mother who is responsible for all our bad luck. Well, these mothers are everything we've ever resented: destructive, rich, snobbish, powerful, and always, always, meddlesome. At worst they hatch evil plots; at best they are deadly gossips. At bottom, they need to take over other peoples' lives. About the only kind thing one can say of them is that they are not so selfish as their actions suggest: whatever they do, it's for somebody's good. There seems to be a need on the part of viewers to believe that there are such characters, and that they're always wrong. Viewers never identify *themselves* with the villainous mother, says one head writer who gets mail on the subject, "but she's just like their mother, or their mother-in-law, or their aunt." We doubt it.

1

2

3

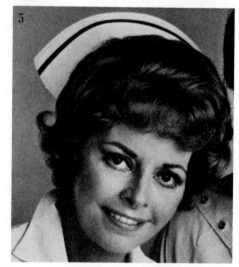

5

The benevolent

1. Bert Bauer (*Guiding Light*)
2. Sarah Caldwell (*Love of Life*)
3. Mona Kane (*All My Children*)
4. Alice Horton (*Days of Our Lives*)
5. Nurse Jessie Brewer (*General Hospital*)
6. Maeve Ryan (*Ryan's Hope*)
7. Kate Martin (*All My Children*)
8. Nancy Hughes (*As the World Turns*)
9. Ellen Stewart (*As the World Turns*))

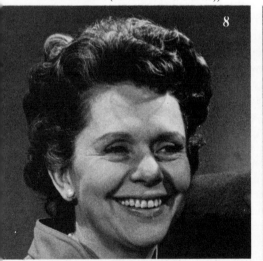

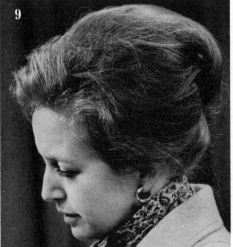

mother/grandmother

These women have seen more than their share of trouble (considering that they are so inoffensive in the first place). But they go right on believing in the sanctity of marriage, the indestructibility of family life, and so on and so forth. Their attitude can be characterized as optimism in the face of the facts— by far the bravest form of optimism. The Benevolent Mother/Grandmother may also be called a "matriarch." If she is not the matriarch of a family, she is, like Jessie Brewer, the matriarch of the soaps' second most important institution—the hospital. She is of a simple and religious nature. She tries to be tolerant and non-interfering with respect to her children; but that's difficult for her since she really does know what's Right.

1. Laura Horton (*Days of Our Lives*) - psychiatrist
2. Pat Randolph (*Another World*) - executive secretary
3. Vicki Paisley (*Somerset*) - executive
4. Amy Kaslo Carson (*Search for Tomorrow*) - doctor
5. Maggie Powers (*The Doctors*) - doctor
6. Sarah McIntyre (Werner) (*Guiding Light*) - doctor
7. Mary Ryan Fenelli (*Ryan's Hope*) - television reporter
8. Lesley Faulkner (*General Hospital*) - doctor
9. Susan Stewart (*As the World Turns*) - doctor
10. Nancy Karr (*Edge of Night*) - newspaper columnist

The career woman

The career woman is not so much an archetype as a role model. She is strongwilled but feminine; successful in her work, but pleasingly vulnerable in love and family life. Although most of the career women are, like their male counterparts, doctors or lawyers, there are novelists, architects, executives and secretaries as well. A list of all soap opera women who work happily outside the home would be so long as to resemble a "Who's Who" for daytime. The Career Women we've chosen are among the more attractive role models, and represent a variety of careers. Aside from their career image, and their good taste in clothes, these women are not necessarily similar in character or dramatic function. They include heroines like Laura Horton and Jill Coleridge, as well as unsympathetic types like Gwen Parish and Vicki Paisley.

6

7

8

9

1

MARRIAGE AND OTHER SEXUAL LIFESTYLES

When Julie and Doug were married this summer (*Days of Our Lives*) one middle-aged fan went out and bought a dress for the occasion. It's true, she "needed it anyhow." And certainly she knew the difference between a real and television event. (The actors, Susan and Bill, had married each other years ago.) But for her, as for other fans, a soap wedding is something in which one participates, something to which one is "invited." From the beginning of soap opera to the present day, weddings of popular characters have drawn enormous response. When Elly and Stu were married (*Search for Tomorrow*) the show received 20,000 congratulatory letters and numerous wedding gifts which were actually used on the show as props.

Soap viewers, young and old, like to see their favorite characters get married. They will wait many years for the happy event—nine years, for example, for Elly and Stu. Producers seem to enjoy weddings too, often going all out in costumes and settings. A recent wedding on *Ryan's Hope* was staged in a Fifth Avenue church, complete with stained glass windows and Catholic litany. When it was over, writer/creator Claire Labine shook her head and said quietly, "They were really married, Mary and Jack." Members of the cast were moved to tears.

Now most romantic tales that do not end in death end in marriage. The soaps recognize this. Writers may keep lovers apart for years and years, but eventually the desires of characters (and viewers) must be consummated at the altar. The problem is that the soaps are open-ended. Unlike other romantic story forms, they must show the morning after—the years after. They must give us the breathless, satisfying ending (the wedding); and there must be no let-up after that. Few forms (and fewer couples) are so ambitious.

The soaps succeed in maintaining interest after marriage. In fact, married life in soapland is as dramatically interesting as premarital courtship—and very often, just about as insecure. It seems that

Julie and Doug Williams (*Days of Our Lives*). Will they live happily ever after?

When Joe Werner (*Guiding Light*) died, his wife Sarah went through a realistic period of grief and mourning, a kind of realism rare in the treatment of this subject. In another unusual plot development, Ben Harper marries Betsy Crawford; she becomes a bride and he becomes a bigamist.

husbands and wives experience the uncertainty and romantic turmoil we tend to associate with the dating years. Lisa and husband number four are a case in point (*As the World Turns*). They recently worked through a traumatic separation, followed by traumatic reconciliation, and a well-deserved second honeymoon. It happened to coincide with their first anniversary! More fortunate couples hang around in a happily married state for years before the inevitable triangle develops and divorce is mentioned. ("A happy marriage is the kiss of death," said one head writer, explaining the phenomenon.) Ruth and Joe Martin (*All My Children*) are a recent example. Ruth's reputation as a chaste, happy, solidly married woman did not deter the writers, or David Thornton, from proposing a "whole new life" for her.

Not only is marriage as uncertain and temporary as courtship— it is just as free; as free, that is, of those real life problems we associate with married life. For example, child care and home-making, the special duties of the married woman are de-emphasized: all the diaper-changing and furniture polishing goes on during commercials. There is little if any connection between the roles of husband and father. And except on shows like *Another World,* breadwinning appears to take place on the side. Few couples face financial problems, bad school systems, or day-care crises. Medical bills for all those long hospital stays are

simply not mentioned; or, if they are (*Ryan's Hope* and *Young and Restless*) hope is held out that some wealthy person connected with the family will pick them up. In-law problems surface now and then, but no more after marriage than before.

There are, it seems, only two kinds of problems that affect married couples more often than unmarried couples. The first is serious illness or disability. Only after Brad and Leslie finally marry does Brad succumb to mysterious bouts of blindness. Again, it is only after marriage to the heroine of the tale that Steve discovers that he is suffering from leukemia (*Search for Tomorrow*) and Jack incurs multiple injuries in an auto accident (*Ryan's Hope*). The soaps see very little point in being ill and single. Illness is a problem that affects the family unit, and is to be shared, in particular, with one's mate.

A second great dilemma that confronts married couples only is of course divorce. Divorce is a major personal problem in the soaps: the Decision to Divorce is the most important decision made by any soap opera character. The decision to so much as mention divorce takes weeks of a character's life and draws many hundreds of letter from troubled viewers. It's not that divorce is so final. (Soap opera characters remarry discarded partners at a rate statistically higher than average.) It's not even that characters and viewers disapprove of divorce in principle. (As we shall see, they do not.) The point is

A happy honeymooning couple. Vicky and Joe Riley of *One Life to Live.*

that divorce is a moral decision—one that has to be justified. Unmarried couples experience painful breakups, but they are not confronted with a difficult moral decision. The decision which confronts the single person—the decision to marry—is itself nothing compared to the decision to divorce; indeed the one is sometimes made with reference to the other. For example, Julie knows that marriage to Doug is the right marriage for her, because it is the *last* marriage for her; she says she walks into that church knowing that this time she won't get divorced. Even in more playful dialogue, characters seem to recognize the importance of passing, in advance, that ultimate test. "What's wrong with you two," says a character on *The Doctors,* "You're not even married and you're headed for divorce."

If marriage more or less resembles courtship, the reverse is also true. Dating relationships tend to be treated very seriously on the soaps. Lovers form the same emotional bonds as married people. And, what is more surprising, they are subject to many of the same social sanctions.

This can be seen in some of the more modern arrangements. Couples do not just sleep together and live together in today's soaps. They undergo some kind of "marriage." Tara and Phil (*All My Children*) married each other "without benefit of clergy" in a chapel shortly before Phil went to Viet Nam. (They managed to have a large conventional

wedding next time around.) Mary and Jack (*Ryan's Hope*) lived together, but not exactly without benefit of clergy. They and the family were counseled throughout by Father McShane and Sister Mary Jo. The issue of commitment was raised day after day, and so heavily that the viewer could hardly help thinking that most people enter into life-long marriages without half that consideration. When Mary and Jack did marry, they had a large and traditional wedding. But not all went smoothly. Guests were stalled in their pews for over two hours as Mary and Jack reviewed their feelings of commitment with Father McShane.

Another young couple who lived together with great seriousness were Trish and Mike (*Days of Our Lives*). This relationship was about as far from marriage as any could be. It was a platonic relationship, recognized as such by the entire community of Salem. Nevertheless, when the arrangement broke up, this was treated as if it were the dissolution of a twenty-year marriage. Trish tried to hide the awful truth from all their mutual acquaintances. Even more bizarre, Grandmother Horton (Mike's grandmother) marched around demanding to know what caused the two to "break up housekeeping." It is clear that the supposed flexibility of the premarital arrangement does not exist for these characters. Other couples who have lived together with great purpose include Brooke

Wanda and Vinnie Wolek have a marriage that lots of us can identify with; they have their spats but the relationship works.

and David (*Days of Our Lives*), John and Jennifer (*Search for Tomorrow*), and Heather and Jerry (*Somerset*).

That the living together arrangement is taken seriously by the community does not mean that it is a respectable substitute for marriage. The goal in most cases *is* marriage. Women usually admit this from the start. Even the men have to come around. Steve Kaslo (*Search for Tomorrow*) wanted to live with Liza, until he "matured" and found his way to the altar. Something similar happened to Jack Fenelli (*Ryan's Hope*). When he complains, in retrospect, that there's something to be said for "living in uncomplicated sin," a friend quips, "As I recall, that didn't work." It never does, on the soaps.

Sleeping or living together without interest in marriage is consequently rare. Even bitter or sophisticated characters who speak out against marriage, desire it in their heart of hearts. Cathy Craig (*One Life to Live*) and Amy Kaslo (*Search for Tomorrow*) both expressed low opinions of the institution of marriage. Both were rewarded with babies out of wedlock; both thereupon offered heroic resistance to marriage, but were in fact so eager that they ended up marrying men who they knew did not love them. (Was their attitude at fault?)

The young woman who prefers a career to marriage is just as unfortunate. Carol Lamonte, ambitious architect, says she has little use for

marriage and children. But other characters point out that she would quickly change her mind if boyfriend Willis would propose (*Another World*). He didn't. In fact, it was only after Carol left town that Willis reformed and began to think positively about marriage—with someone else. Carol's career-girl stance is seen as defensive and unattractive.

Even worse is the attitude displayed by Martha McGee (*Ryan's Hope*), a minor character who might be seen as a caricature of the "modern" woman. Martha is a high-powered reporter who doesn't feel the need to commit herself to anything besides her work. She believes in sex without emotional consequences. ("I'm not sure you're my heart's desire, but you're sexy as hell," she says at one point to the incredulous Jack Fenelli.) According to Martha the idea of waiting for the Right Man is "wasting time" and she hates to waste time. A lot of girls feel that way, she claims. Well, not on the soaps they don't. Fenelli points out that there are "a lot of Cinderellas disguised as sophisticated ladies," which means they all want marriage underneath. He seems to be right: Cinderella wins out in this case, and Martha, super-reporter, is left sobbing in a phone booth. The soaps want no part of her philosophy. Nor is her type dramatically useful in the romantic storyline. Where there's no emotional commitment, there's no conflict. Where there are casual relationships, there is no handwringing.

Carla and Ed Hall of *One Life to Live* (left); she's stubborn but he still wears pants in the family. Liza and Steve Kaslo of *Search for Tomorrow* (right); love conquers all, including (probably) his leukemia.

Sleeping around doesn't serve any point, because it just doesn't produce the necessary tension between two people.

The soaps are about *commitment,* in and out of marriage, but especially within marriage. They are concerned about what makes marriage "work," and what makes it come apart. Critics may complain that marriages fail with depressing regularity—that all is domestic disaster—but they would be hard put to come up with a more realistic view of marital trials. Though the divorce statistics may be way out of line on a given program, or a husband may occasionally depart for unconvincing reasons (such as the actor's need to pursue a Hollywood career), marital breakup and reconciliation is usually portrayed in a realistic, even helpful way.

A significant point (and sometimes a criticism) is that "good marriages" are just as likely to fail as others. Couples like Pat and John Randolph (*Another World*), Ruth and Joe Martin (*All My Children*), and Eunice and John Wyatt (*Search for Tomorrow*) are held up for years as models. The couple dispenses advice and comfort to others. Then one day, they too are in serious trouble. Other characters are overcome with disbelief. Grandmotherly types wring their hands and say things like, "I just don't understand how a relationship that has been so good for so long can deteriorate." Other characters remind themselves

that "nobody knows what goes on between two people." The seemingly arbitrary breakup of the seemingly "perfect" couple is dismissed by critics as typical "soap opera" stuff ("a world of fly apart marriages, throw away husbands..."). But we all know it's realistic enough. Especially since the problems experienced by the couple are plausible, ordinary problems that in fact account for a large share of marital failures.

When a "good marriage" fails on the soaps, the problem is usually "lack of communication," an inability of one partner to share his life with the other. (A recent extensive study by the Family Service Association of America shows that poor communication *is* the single most important cause of marital failure—so the soaps are entirely realistic here.) In some cases, the communication problems are obvious, and a little silly. A wife goes running off without waiting to hear her husband's perfectly sound explanation; a husband hides information which it makes no sense to hide. For example Brad (*Young and Restless*) does not tell his wife Leslie that he is going blind. Instead he makes mysterious trips to a Chicago clinic, creating suspicion and distrust in his marriage. As blindness is something no one can hide for long, one hopes that Brad will one day walk in the door with a seeing eye dog and a full explanation. Instead he has asked his wife for a divorce.

Scheming Phoebe Tyler of *All My Children* (left) still can't understand why her husband wants to leave a superior person like herself. Rachel, softened by the love of husband Mac Cory, lovingly sculpts his likeness—but he is jealous of the time she spends in the studio.

A more realistic (or perhaps more common) kind of communication failure in marriage is illustrated by Pat and John Randolph (*Another World*) and Ruth and Joe Martin (*All My Children*). In these marriages the communication failure is more general; no one misunderstanding occurs, but gradually the couple grows apart. Finally, they have little life in common. "I left you because you didn't tell me what was going on with our children," says John Randolph, "*You never trusted me enough to make me part of your life.*" Strikingly similar language is used to describe the marital difficulties experienced by other "good" couples.

When a wife doesn't trust her husband enough to make him *part of her life,* or vice versa, one or both partners in the marriage are likely to develop extramarital interests. On the soaps people come together out of "common loneliness"; and there is apparently no greater loneliness than that which is felt by a neglected spouse. Forced separation, over-dedication to a career, and disagreements over children are among the factors that lead to silence, then loneliness, and the inevitable affair. The soaps do not contend that loneliness is a justification for adultery. It is merely motivation (that is, justification for the storyline). A number of scenes will show a husband feeling "not part of his wife's life"—and soon another woman will enter. Kevin is shown to be unhappy over his wife's nightly devotion to her studies (*Edge of Night*) and the viewer is thereby prepared to accept the entrance of Dr. Chris Neely. Mac Cory is shown to be depressed over Rachel's single-minded dedication to her sculpture (*Another World*), and the viewer is prepared for a series of jealous misunderstandings. Husbands who neglect their wives (for example, Frank Ryan, *Ryan's Hope;* Joe Martin, *All My Children*) can also expect to encounter rivals. It is made clear that the wife in such instances would have preferred her husband, had he seemed interested in her at the proper moment. Unfortunately, another man needed her, appreciated her, more.

In most instances of this sort, the extra-marital affair is treated not as a thing in itself, but as a symptom of a a failing marriage. The wayward heroine makes it clear that sex was the last thing on her mind. Sympathetic characters simply do not lose their heads; they do not have affairs out of sexual need, or what used to be called the Grand Passion. In fact, the kind of affairs they have may not be sexual at all. The female character may declare her intention to keep things on an "emotional" level; or the writer may be so ambiguous that no viewer could swear that sexual intercourse is taking place. The sympathetic character has an affair because she needs someone to talk to—because she is lonely. Sexual attachment, if it does take place, surprises all

The marriage of Mary Ryan and Jack Fenelli (*Ryan's Hope*) is precariously balanced. They really love each other; but are they right together?

parties.

In good marriages, the break is usually due to communication failure, leading to loneliness and isolation in the marriage, and sometimes, to extramarital affairs. In bad or questionable marriages, reasons for failure are somewhat different. Here a big reason is out-and-out deception. Husbands like John Dixon (*As the World Turns*) lie, cheat, and blackmail in order to keep their wives. Unsympathetic female characters are more likely to deceive men into marrying them in the first place. A woman may fake pregnancy or lie about the paternity of her child. When she's found out, the marriage is understandably in trouble. A really bad sort of woman will break up a true love relationship (intercepting messages or misrepresenting events) so as to catch a man on the "rebound." For example, Iris, in order to marry Robert Delaney, prevents him from finding out that Clarice is pregnant with his child (*Another World*). Robert is so enraged by the deception that he slashes Iris's portrait, and deserts her altogether.

Deceptions about feeling (for example, marrying for money and calling it love) and deceptions about one's past may cause marital trouble for the less sympathetic character. Unwarranted suspicions about infidelity are also common. Phyllis divorced Bob Anderson (*Days of Our Lives*) because she thought he was having an affair with Julie (he wasn't). On the same show, Mickey had an affair with Linda Patterson Phillips because he thought wife Laura was having an affair with brother Bill (she wasn't). Divorce naturally followed. Since sexual events are far less important than emotional factors, it hardly matters whether people are really having affairs. Mistrust and deceptions of all kinds are at the base of marital discord among the unsympathetic characters.

When a marriage is in trouble, divorce will generally be mentioned. The soaps are philosophically opposed to divorce—but dramatically, they could not live without it. Even among the traditional Catholics of *Ryan's Hope*, the possibility of divorce must exist, says writer/creator Paul Avila Mayer; it is necessary to storytelling.

Still, divorce must be introduced very carefully. It must be justified in moral terms, especially on the more traditional soaps. "We recognize on the show that marriages do fail, but by the same token we don't treat marriage lightly," says Joe Willmore, Producer of *As the World Turns,* "For example, when Kim Dixon divorced her husband John it was a justified act, perhaps overly justified." The more sympathetic the character, the more justification is needed. Selfish motives and sexual preferences do not enter into it.

Generally the character can defend her decision by proving to viewers that she has tried to make her

Diana and Peter Taylor (*General Hospital*) have both had more than their share of problems, but they find comfort in each other.

marriage work. Among the most common lines in all of soapland are, "I want to make my marriage work," or "I am fighting to save my marriage." Virtually everybody respects this sentiment. Even poor Peggy Brooks, in love with a married man, defends his wife for trying to keep him: she is only trying to make her marriage work, explains Peggy to the husband in question. Peggy goes so far as to help her rival, urging her to pick out pretty dresses and play the Total Woman game—for only if she fights for that marriage, and loses, can Peggy move in on her husband without guilt. The moral of this preposterous tale is that a woman who fights for her marriage must be accorded respect, even if she's your rival. If you don't fight and fight hard, you are not in a position to object to, or institute, divorce. In most cases, "fighting for one's marriage," or "making marriage work" requires compromise, forgiveness, sacrifices, and increased efforts at honest communication. Often it requires a willingness to seek help from a marriage counselor, psychologist, or family member. Only after all such strategies fail—or after one or another of the partners has proved himself a villain beyond all doubt—can divorce be reasonably considered.

The Decision to Divorce is, of course, treated at some length. For people in the real world, this decision is gravely affected by feelings about children; by finances; and, of course, by fears of loneliness. In the soaps these concerns are not quite so important. In particular, the fear of loneliness—the fear of making one's way again as a single person—is insignificant. The divorced soap opera character can expect to be quickly entangled in a new love relationship. (Problems of widowhood are overlooked in the same heartless manner!) The Decision to Divorce is not so much a decision to do without a certain husband, or to acquire another one; it is more significantly a decision to break up a home and extended family. Many soap characters point out this difference. Delia (*Ryan's Hope*) continually says that she fears losing not only her husband, but the Ryans' and her identity. Ruth, explaining what the breakdown of her marriage means, says softly, "*It's so much more than Joe.* It's sitting on the porch with Kate...the sound of children...the smell of honeysuckle..." Joe hardly figures in it—and why should he in a world where new husbands materialize very quickly?

When the Decision to Divorce is made, and divorce is imminent, characters and viewers seem to feel called upon to pass judgment, to take sides. Many letters are received by the character who wants the divorce. "When I divorced Natalie," says C. David Colson, "I got a letter from a woman in Ohio..." and he describes a curious mixture of hate-mail rhetoric and religious dogma on the sanctity of marriage. When a long-married couple breaks up, the show

The traditional "good" marriage is exemplified by Maeve and Johnny Ryan, heads of the Ryan clan (right). The problems of modern marriage are shown in the tangled relationship of Ben and Betsy Harper (*Love of Life*).

receives more thoughtful letters. Some viewers chastise the writers for breaking up a beautiful couple—a couple they had faith in. Others cheer on the defecting partner, saying things like, "Let that woman have herself a good time!" Although the soaps operate on the assumption that marriage must be preserved whenever possible, viewer response to the failure of long-term marriages is not so conservative. Budd Kloss, producer of *All My Children,* says that the mail was 50-50 in favor of Ruth's divorcing Joe, for example.

There are, however, some marriages which simply can't break up. These are marriages of older, wiser characters, the matriarchs and patriarchs who uphold the values of family life. Among these are Alice and Tom Horton (*Days of Ours Lives*), Anna and Jim Craig (*One Life to Live*), Vanessa and Bruce Sterling (*Love of Life*), Maggie and Matt Powers (*The Doctors*), Maeve and Johnny Ryan (*Ryan's Hope*) and Ellen and David Stewart, and Nancy and Chris Hughes (*As the World Turns*). Though these marriages appear to be invincible, they are not "perfect." There are always problems. For example, Vanessa Sterling has had to forgive Bruce for several affairs; and Alice and Tom Horton sometimes disagree on what should be done with respect to their bizarre and troubled household. Still, these characters tend to express their doubts and fears, and settle the problem. If there is any forgiving to be

done (as for example in the Sterling marriage) the women are strong and ready. With the rest of the family in disarray, one supposes that stability in marriage is an emotional necessity for these characters. Again, the marriage is seen as part of an extended family structure. It is not a partnership between two self-interested, self-actualizing people, but rather a partnership charged with providing care and comfort to other family members. "Thank you for taking care of my father all these years," says Chris Hughes to Nancy upon the death of Grandpa Hughes. "He was mine, too," she answers softly. This kind of sentiment prevails on the younger, trendier soaps as well; it is, if anything, thicker on *Ryan's Hope,* one of the newest soaps.

Few viewers of the soaps set out to emulate Nancy and Chris Hughes or Alice and Tom Horton. Most identify with younger lovers. Most expect (and enjoy) a sentimental wedding at the end of the storyline. ("Will Tara and Phil ever make it to the altar?" fans always asked Agnes Nixon, knowing full well that marriage will by no means end their problems—will probably make no difference whatsoever!) The soaps must have it both ways. Marriage as the romantic answer to our dreams. Marriage as the practical, working problem of our lives. If it's a contradiction, it's one we're used to living with.

THE THREE SIDES OF LOVE

The love triangle. Two women in love with the same man. Two men in love with the same woman. Consider the possible complications. Three people whose lives are in some way torn by an impossible situation. From the beginning of the written word, the subject has fascinated us. One of the earliest examples is in the Bible. King David, in love with Bathsheba, uses his powers and position to send her husband to the front lines of battle where he is killed.

The story of David and Bathsheba, a tragic moral tale, is but one of the countless possibilities of the love triangle. Over the centuries, a triangle has been at the heart of tales of revenge such as Euripides' "The Medea," tales of the imperfection of the human condition such as the Legend of King Arthur, Queen Guinevere, and Sir Lancelot; and yes, the love triangle has even been funny. In Restoration comedies and French farces of the 1890s, there is nothing so common as the doting elderly husband who is unaware of the lover his wife has stashed in the bedroom closet.

The love triangle came into daytime serials at the beginning. It was natural. In the antique radio soap, *The Romance of Helen Trent*, there was a permanent triangle; Helen, an ever-present suitor Gil, and the many unusually evil men with whom Helen would fall temporarily in love.

The best known love triangle in television soap opera was on *Another World*. For years, Steven Frame vacillated between Rachel and Alice. Rachel appealed to Steve's darker nature, but more importantly, she was there first—an important claim in most love triangles. Alice appealed to Steve's better inclinations. When she appeared, Rachel hung on, tearing all three of them in the process (see next page). No conflict in soap opera was quite so popular as this. Three people. Two women in love with the same man. A love triangle. A variation of a story that runs through our literature because it has so many possibilities— possibilities that have been used to full advantage in daytime serial drama.

Steven Frame
Rachel Frame
Alice Matthews
ANOTHER WORLD

Steven Frame was a self-made man who had risen from a poverty stricken family to become a wealthy member of the Bay City community, and owner of Frame Enterprises. Rachel Davis, a beautiful and bored young woman from a background similar to Steve's, began to take an interest in him. Rachel wanted Steve for the money and power he could give her, and she threw herself at him at every opportunity. Steve wasn't very interested in Rachel, but one night they slept together. That turned out to be Steve's biggest mistake. Rachel became pregnant.

At this point the triangle began to form. Steve fell in love with lovely Alice Matthews a decidedly 'good' girl, from a good family. Steve tried to keep Rachel's pregnancy a secret, believing that Alice would never marry him if she learned the truth. Villainous Rachel saw to it that she did. Alice left for Europe to mend her broken heart but upon returning, became Mrs. Steven Frame. Meanwhile, Rachel had married Russ Matthews and convinced him that the baby was his. Eventually Russ learned the truth and divorced Rachel. Rachel married Ted Clark, but later divorced him. She began to see Steve without Alice's knowledge—

using their son, Jamie, as bait. Alice became pregnant, and one night, while Steve was visiting Rachel and Jamie, Alice lost her child. Once again she was heartbroken when she learned that Steve had been with Rachel. She assumed they were having an affair, and instead of confronting Steve, ran away to New York. She divorced Steve, who, upon being so abandoned, married Rachel. Alice later returned to Bay City and she and Steve had a heart-to-heart. Realizing he'd been duped by Rachel, Steve sued for divorce. To insure that the divorce would be granted, he bribed Rachel's father. Steve's lawyer found out about it and reported it to the courts. The divorce was granted, but Steve was later sent to prison for six months—after he remarried Alice.

Everything looked rosy for the newlyweds: they were together, Rachel was being romanced by wealthy Mac Cory, and Steve's business was doing very well. Then Steve went on a business trip and never came back. Alice had decided to adopt a little girl, Sally, and wired Steve about it. On his way home his helicopter crashed and Alice was left a shocked and heartbroken widow. (But Steve's body was never ever found...)

...a classic love triangle

Phil Brent
Tara Martin
Chuck Tyler
ALL MY CHILDREN

Phil and Tara were childhood sweethearts, but Fate has continually interfered to keep them apart. Learning that his real father was Nick Davis, Phil developed amnesia and wandered off to New York. He later returned to find his true love about to marry Chuck, simply because she was angry and hurt about having been abandoned. Nick Davis stopped the wedding and Phil and Tara began their relationship anew. But before the lovers could marry—before they could do anything but say their vows in an empty church—Phil was drafted and sent to Viet Nam. Tara then discovered that she was pregnant with Phil's child (little Phil). Phil was reported missing in action and, to give her child a father, Tara agreed to marry Chuck. That marriage might have worked if Phil hadn't returned to find his true love married to another man. In time, Phil found out little Phil was his son and he and Tara made plans to marry. Tara divorced Chuck but once again Fate intervened. This time, little Phil, unable to cope with his parents' break-up, developed a psychosomatic illness—severe asthma attacks. The wedding was once again postponed until the boy could accept Phil as his stepfather, and until Tara could work through her guilt. Finally Tara came to realize that if she felt secure in marrying Phil, little Phil would come around. So far he hasn't. No one is seen as the villain in this triangle, since all are relatively good and decent people. Sympathies lie with Tara and Phil because of their "beautiful love," but the wealthy, handsome, idealistic Chuck has had his fair share of viewer sympathy as well. Most viewers would like to see him happy—but with someone else.

David Thornton
Ruth Martin
Joe Martin
ALL MY CHILDREN

Ruth and Joe Martin made the perfect, happy couple. For years they provided advice, a shoulder to cry on, and a helping hand to everyone in Pine Valley. But when David Thornton arrived in town, things changed. David felt drawn to Ruth: he admired her, respected her, and began to fall in love with her. Ruth was careful not to give David any encouragement even though she was equally charmed by him. The romance might not have come to the surface were it not for two factors: Joe's busy schedule at the hospital (which led him to neglect his wife) and Joe's daughter's romance with Ruth's son (the Tara/Phil relationship). Joe blamed Ruth for destroying Tara's marriage to Chuck by telling Phil that he (not Chuck) was the father of little Phil. Ruth and Joe had many a bitter argument and Ruth turned to David for comfort and advice. David in turn confided in Ruth, telling her of the painful experiences that led him to forsake a career as a surgeon and work instead as a hospital aide. Ruth tried to make a go of her marriage, but found herself becoming emotionally involved with the kind, gentle (and persistent) David. Joe learned what was going on and was very hurt by his wife's "friendship" with David. Then Ruth moved out of the Martin home in order to have time to think things over. Still Joe couldn't believe that Ruth could be in love with David, and thought that the relationship would end. It didn't seem that way until Joe had to have a dangerous emergency appendectomy. At that point Ruth realized that she loved Joe; David realized that she loved Joe; and everyone else realized that they had known it all along! An interesting twist was that David Thornton was forced to forsake his disguise and perform the emergency surgery on Joe. (No one else was around to save Joe's life!) Now that David is recognized as a doctor and has received a job offer, he should feel secure enough to be able to do without Ruth. It seems their relationship was based on his needs all along. Viewer sympathy was split pretty evenly between Joe and David while the conflict lasted.

Nicole Drake
Adam Drake
Brandy Henderson
THE EDGE OF NIGHT

Adam and Nicole went through hell and highwater before they were married. Things had finally settled down for the lovers and they went to the Caribbean for their long-awaited honeymoon. But the forces of evil followed them. In order to stop Adam from running for state senator, the underworld blew up the boat Adam and Nicole were on. Adam survived, but there wasn't a trace of Nicole. Heartbroken, Adam returned home. After months of grief, he found comfort in the arms of District Attorney Brandy Henderson. Their relationship grew, until Adam, giving up any hope of ever finding his beloved Nicole again, asked Brandy to marry him. Then, Nicole was found, suffering from amnesia. She returned home, uncertain of her relationship with Adam after so many months. After a bad start, Adam and Nicole got back together again. Brandy was bitter about losing Adam and began publicly stating that she hated Nicole and wished her dead. But it proved to be an empty threat; though Brandy still loves Adam, she has come to realize the Adam loves Nicole. Viewer sympathy lies with Nicole and Adam because theirs is the longer lasting relationship and perhaps because Brandy is a career woman able to handle herself, come what may. Nicole appears to be a more steady, more loving, and less aggressive woman than Brandy. But both Brandy and Nicole have elicited viewer symphathy.

Jillian Coleridge
Frank Ryan
Delia Ryan
RYAN'S HOPE

Frank Ryan turned to the intelligent and sensitive Jillian Coleridge when it became clear that his marriage to childish, selfish Delia was a disaster. Delia was set against his career as a politician and took no interest in him at all. Through a series of mishaps, Frank's affair became known right before his election bid for city councilman. Delia was furious. In order to keep Frank for herself, Delia saved his political career by telling everyone that they had reconciled. In a corner, Frank agreed to the charade. In time, he and Delia began to make their marriage work. But it wasn't quick enough for Delia, who still felt rejected by Frank. To ease her anguish, she turned to Jill's brother, Roger Coleridge. The affair between them went on until Delia realized that she did indeed love Frank. But Roger was not about to let go. And on the eve of yet another Frank Ryan election bid (this time for Congressman), Roger contrived to spill the beans and ruin Frank's career. He also ruined Frank and Delia's marriage. When Frank found out about Delia's affair, and her multiple deceptions, he walked out on her and resumed his affair with Jill, who had never stopped loving him. Frank hopes to marry Jill should he be so fortunate as to be able to divorce Delia. This will not be easy, because the simple Jill/Frank/Delia triangle has begot new triangles with their own problems. Delia is playing on Pat Ryan's old tender feelings for her, and Jill must come to terms with her feelings for Seneca Beaulac, to whom she briefly became attached during Frank's long absence and whose child she is carrying, unbeknownst to Frank. Delia is the villain of this piece—but she's not a viscious villain. She's merely an immature girl, conniving, spoiled, and possibly dangerous. Viewer sympathy lies with whomever she comes in contact with (even bad Roger is seen, sympathetically, as her dupe). Viewer sympathy also occasionally lies with Delia because she cries and pleads her case so well.

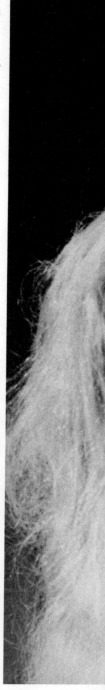

Greg Peters
Amanda Howard
Neil Curtis
DAYS OF OUR LIVES

Amanda Howard found herself falling for Dr. Neil Curtis when the grief over her husband's death finally faded. The two were set to marry when (the night before the wedding), Amanda discovered Neil with another woman. Amanda's friends had warned her that Dr. Curtis was a ladies' man, a gambler, an unreliable sort, but she hadn't listened. Shattered by her discovery, Amanda fled. She was later found in the woods, suffering from overexposure to the cold. Greg Peters became her protector and doctor, and he found himself falling in love. His marriage to Susan Peters was on the rocks and the beautiful and naive Amanda needed him. Susan and Greg were divorced, leaving him free to marry Amanda. But Amanda had never gotten over Neil. Only when Neil married Phyllis Anderson did Amanda lose hope of ever marrying him. She accepted Greg's proposal, while remaining good friends with Neil. Though still in love with Neil, she also loved Greg. Then a brain operation was performed on Amanda and she developed amnesia. Neither Greg nor Neil wanted to tell her about their special relationship to her, but both men were at her side throughout her ordeal. Both men were there too as she slowly regained her memory. Greg, it seems, won out. In a bitter tirade, Amanda told Neil she hated him for what he'd done to her—and said she never wanted to see him again. Since the two work in the same hospital, that was an unrealistic request. Amanda's subsequent marriage to Greg may turn out to be just as unrealistic. This triangle has not been resolved and probably won't be for several years. No one is really the villain here—and it's unclear where viewer sympathy lies.

Dan Stewart
Kim Dixon
John Dixon
AS THE WORLD TURNS

Kim Reynolds married John Dixon because she needed a father for her baby and because John was determined to have her for his very own. When Kim lost the baby and her marriage seemed hopeless (she did try and make a go of it), she asked John for a divorce. He refused and tried to blackmail her into staying with him. Their marriage continued to drag on after John's threat became pointless. Kim had decided to leave John again when he fell down some stairs. He begged her to stay with him until he was well. Kim did, only to fall in love with John's doctor, Dan Stewart. When John and Dan's ex-wife Susan, learned of the romance, they tried to destroy it. John tried to make Kim feel guilty by telling her she would destroy Susan if she ever tried to marry Dan. Kim left town to think things over. However, during her short vacation, a tornado struck the town and Kim was injured. The injury led to amnesia, which John decided to take advantage of. He kept visitors away from Kim and told her only that he was her husband (and not about the state of their marriage). When Kim's memory finally returned, she called Dan—but the call was intercepted by Susan. So neither Dan nor Kim knew how concerned the other was. Dan felt Kim didn't love him any longer, and Kim felt that Dan had gotten tired of waiting for her. Both continued on their separate and eventful paths. Recently Dan married Valerie Conway. Obviously Dan and Kim have not gotten back together. Yet there are many in Oakdale who feel that nothing can stop them from eventually finding happiness with each other. John Dixon is the villain in this love triangle, as is Susan Stewart. But Fate (in form of the tornado) is also a major factor in keeping the lovers apart.

**Cal Aleata
Rick Latimer
Meg Hart**
LOVE OF LIFE

After an unfortunate romance with young David Hart, Cal found herself turning to older Rick Latimer. Her mother, Meg, was already involved with Rick, but everyone thought they were just business partners. Meg tried to destroy the romance; she thought she could control Rick since she held the pursestrings for their mutual business—"Beaver Ridge." Meg's tactics succeeded for a time. But Rick found Cal's innocence refreshing and fell in love with her. Rick found Meg attractive too—a haughty, independent woman, quite unlike her daughter. Rick became engaged to Cal but continued trying to keep Meg at bay. Finally, Meg threatened to tell her daughter about the affair with Rick. Threatened with exposure, Rick broke the engagement. But Cal was persistent. The two made plans to elope. Meg found out about it and told her daughter all. Heartbroken, Cal rushed off to San Francisco to forget her mother and Rick. But when Rick appeared with a proposal of marriage this became difficult. Cal accepted his proposal, whereupon Meg attempted suicide. However, Cal and Rick married anyhow, and even Meg was happy. She feels that Rick, once married to Cal will realize she's nothing but a child, and will come running back to a mature woman—herself. Meg is the villain, not only of this triangle, but of the show as well. Rick, however, is not blameless and his past is sordid. The only person who really has the audience's sympathy is Cal, the eternal innocent. Rick's saving grace is that he truly loves Cal. Meg, too, has her excuses: she's afraid her daughter will get hurt, and after all, she found Rick first.

Jennifer Pace
John Wyatt
Eunice Wyatt
SEARCH FOR TOMORROW

Eunice and John Wyatt's marriage was going through some bad times as a result of Eunice's sexual problems. John turned to Jennifer Pace, a beautiful younger woman, for comfort. He and Jennifer had an affair, which Eunice eventually discovered. John was determined to save his marriage and broke off his relationship with Jennifer. But Jennifer, an extremely insecure and clinging young woman, wouldn't let go. She was constantly visiting John's office, begging him to come back. Eunice usually walked in when they were together and no amount of explaining could convince her that the affair had ended. Finally, Jennifer called John, told him that someone had tried to rape her in her apartment and begged him to come over and protect her. John consequently spent the night on her couch. Eunice found out about it and didn't believe his version of the story. John moved out. Eunice soon realized that she was wrong and was going to try for a reconciliation—until she found out that John had moved in with Jennifer. Eunice filed for divorce, even though she still loved John. John, meanwhile, found out that Jennifer had lied, and that no one had attacked her on that fateful night. Again he packed his bags. He and Eunice patched up their marriage and were back to being like newlyweds. Jennifer attempted suicide; she survived, but as a result went slightly crazy. She kept hearing John talking to her, telling her he loved her, and that he wanted her to kill Eunice so they could marry. All in Jennifer's head, of course. Still Jennifer stole a gun and shot and killed Eunice! Viewer sympathy lies with Eunice, in the grave.

Laura Horton
Bill Horton
Mickey Horton
DAYS OF OUR LIVES

Laura and Bill fell in love while they were both interns. But Bill left town, *and* Laura, when he discovered that a problem with his hands rendered him incapable of being a surgeon. Soon enough Laura and Bill's brother Mickey were thrown together at Susan Martin's murder trial (Mickey was Susan's lawyer, Laura was her psychiatrist). Laura and Mickey married. Thus, when Bill returned to Salem he found his true love married to his brother. Bill tried to forget Laura, but one night, in a drunken stupor, he raped her. Laura discovered she was pregnant, but kept the child's true origins to herself (Mickey, it is known, is sterile). Later, Bill went to prison for manslaughter. (Kitty Horton threatened to tell Mickey that he was not the father of young Michael, whereupon she and Bill fought and Kitty died of heart failure.) Bill returned from prison and Laura learned how Bill had tried unselfishly to protect Mickey from the truth. They were still very much in love, but decided there was nothing they could do without hurting Mickey. However, Mickey suspected that they were having an affair and, as revenge, had an affair with his secretary, Linda Patterson. Laura decided to file for a divorce, but changed her mind when young Michael was hit by a car. As the result of blood typing at the hospital, Mickey realized he couldn't be the boy's father, and had a heart attack. Bill saved his life, but Mickey was unable to cope with the situation and had a stroke. He subsequently wandered away from the hospital. Meanwhile, Bill and Laura grew closer and closer. Assuming Mickey was dead, they married. Mickey turned up later on, suffering from amnesia and married to Maggie, a farm girl. All would have gone well, but Mickey regained his memory when Michael was injured (a truck fell on him). The past came tumbling back and Mickey's mind snapped: he tried to kill Bill. Mickey was sent to a sanitarium, where he refused Maggie as his wife, and continued to think he was married to Laura. He has since been released—perhaps prematurely. Mickey remains bitter about his life, and blames his brother for taking his wife and child away from him. No one is really seen as the villain in this triangle. Viewer sympathy lies with Bill and Laura—they are unselfish, sacrificing, and idealistic. What's more, Bill and Laura were in love long before Mickey appeared on the scene. However, Mickey has suffered too, and much sympathy is lavished on him on screen. In fact, Bill has become jealous of the attention his brother continues to receive, particularly from his guilt-ridden wife.

PARENTS AND CHILDREN

Doug and Julie (*Days of Our Lives*) are seated at a quiet table at "Doug's Place." They are discussing a third character who has been beset by many problems, and is, in the usual course of things, pregnant. After recounting the worst, Julie sighs and says, Well, at least she still has her baby to live for. "Until it grows up and rejects her," says Doug.

Only a few minutes later we hear another intimate conversation on this theme. Grandparents Alice and Tom Horton are disturbed by the behavior of young Mike. After noting that "our children were brought up to honor their fathers and mothers," the two are suddenly contrite. How can he honor us when we have lied and deceived him? they ask each other. How can he *not* reject us?

In the soaps, as in life, parent-child relationships are beset by problems that cannot be easily resolved. The soaps do not "side" with either generation. Although soap commercials nearly always ask us to identify with a youngish mother figure, the drama speaks to us as mothers and daughters, fathers and sons. Sometimes the viewer identifies with a character who represents his own generation—but not always. College students joyfully identify with Mona as she lectures daughter Erica (*All My Children*). And middle-aged parents have no difficulty in sympathizing with characters like Tony (*Somerset*) who have been wronged by their elders.

Generation conflicts enlist our sympathies because they speak to our experience. We may not know what it is like to fall in love several times a year, or to suffer amnesia, rape, or blackmail. But most of us know what it's like to suffer a meddlesome parent, or an ungrateful child. The soaps show this—and happier relationships as well.

It is difficult to generalize about parent-child relationships in soap opera, for they are as varied as those we find in life. Still, some generalizations can be made: One is that there are very few young children, and fewer still are mean, nasty or ugly. Children are talked about more than they are seen. Adults worry about them, fight over them, and debate their parentage. But there are few scenes in which we see a parent locked in emotional conflict with a school-age child. This is one of the areas of life that isn't often presented in the soaps (perhaps because the viewer would have a difficult time deciding whom to identify with).

Another generalization is that grandparents are good people in the old family mold. Kate (*All My Children*) and Sarah (*Love of Life*)

Michael and Hope Bauer (*Guiding Light*) typify the good father/daughter relationship.

are seen as solid, middle-class matriarchs with a deep commitment to family life. They usually articulate the kind of morality we are supposed to approve of and accept. Kate, for example, is always trusting that whatever has come between two people can be worked out, that "nothing is ever gained by separation," and much is gained by staying together. Grandmotherly women like Kate and Sarah are usually not judgmental or interfering. "I must stay out of it," says Kate, characteristically, about her son's problems: and she almost does. Grandfathers in the same reassuring mold include Dr. Charles Tyler (*All My Children*) and Dr. Tom Horton (*Days of Our Lives*).

This is not to suggest that there are no conflicts between grandparents and their grown children. Phoebe (*All My Children*) and Mona (*The Doctors*) happen to be grandmothers—and they are very manipulative women. Their children naturally resent them. It is worth noting that the grandmother role is, in such cases, de-emphasized. Phoebe and Mona are portrayed as upper-class

The warmest families seem to be the poor ones. Thus Maeve Ryan and her daughter Mary (*left*) and Carrie Lovett and her daughter Arlene (*right*) both have close, caring relationships.

socialites, and only secondarily as mothers and grandmothers. The difference is visually apparent. Kate, the good grandmother, is seen mostly in her kitchen, whereas (for all we know) Phoebe does not even have a kitchen. She's seen in boutiques, restaurants, and even in a blond wig! Grandparents seen as grandparents tend to be good; it's only when they are social movers in their own right that they create trouble for their children.

This leads to a third generalization, this one about the effects of money on the parent-child relationship. It seems that money gets in the way of trust and understanding. The rich use money to bribe, wheedle, and defeat their grown children. Phoebe does this (*All My Children*); so do Meg (*Love of Life*), Rex (*Somerset*), and Geraldine (*Edge of Night*). Even with younger dependent children, the rich are not so warm and sympathetic as the poor. Wealthy Iris (*Another World*) cannot hold the affection of her fifteen-year-old son; in fact, she cannot even persuade him to live with her. Seldom do we find such behavior among more ordinary folk. Poor families stick together because they have to. The contrast seems to be intentionally developed. For example, when Meg confronts the much poorer Carrie Lovett (*Love of Life*), she makes a point of envying Carrie because her daughter (though no angel) cares. The implication is that Carrie and Arlene Lovett must stick together through their troubles, because they've had so little.

A similar point is made in a storyline involving Kay and Brock Chancellor (*Young and Restless*). When mother and son both have plenty of money, they have very little need of one another. Only when Brock loses everything does he come back home (and then his mother is suspicious of him, figuring that he's after her money). It takes a while before both understand that what Brock really needs is support and affection. As they achieve this understanding, money becomes less important. In fact, Brock starts urging his mother to give some of it away—to Senior Citizens programs and other

community services. Rex and Tony Cooper (*Somerset*) work through a similar problem. Only when Rex discovers that money won't buy his son or his career can he and Tony begin to develop a real relationship.

In families that are neither rich nor socially prominent, generation conflict must be traced to other causes. What do parent and child fight about?

Professional rivalry is one source of conflict. Given the limited number of occupations that seem open to soap opera men, it is inevitable that many sons will follow in their fathers' footsteps. Usually this is a comfortable arrangement: close father-son pairs who are also professional colleagues include Tom and Bill (*Days of Our Lives*), Joe and Jeff (*All My Children*), and David and Dan (*As the World Turns*). However, professional rivalry does add to the animosity that exists between Matt Powers and his son Mike (*The Doctors*). Matt is an upstanding member of the community, but

Good grandmother Ellen Stewart (*As The World Turns*) helps Betsy with her homework. On the stormier side, professional rivals Dr. Matt Powers and his son, Dr. Mike (*The Doctors*), hide a deep affection for one another under their constant animosity.

Mike, stubborn and sometimes selfish, has had a rougher time of it. Since both men are doctors, Mike is put in the position of trying to live up to his father's good name—a large problem for him. Other sons who have the same problem are Rex (*Somerset*), Roger (*Ryan's Hope*), and Draper (*Edge of Night*).

Inasmuch as the main business of the soaps is romance, many other conflicts are over marital or premarital attachments. Eileen (*One Life to Live*), Phoebe (*All My Children*), Iris (*Another World*), and Johnny (*Ryan's Hope*) are examples of parents who have alienated their children by attempting to wreck a love relationship. (Usually the relationship is only temporarily frustrated.) In other cases, parents oppose their children over divorce decisions or extramarital affairs. But this cuts both ways. College-age Marianne (*Another World*) opposes mother over *her* divorce; and she is vehemently set against mother's new boyfriend. Marianne's twin Michael is equally enraged at his father, and the two are told, as

Bert Bauer (*Guiding Light*) and Tara Tyler (*All My Children*) both know what it is to sacrifice their own needs to those of a much-loved son, and the relationships remain warm and rewarding.

many a parent is told, "Why don't you just stop judging [them] and let them work things out for themselves!"

Seldom is such good advice taken, and so it is that many conflicts result from parents' interference in their children's love affairs, and vice versa. There are the usual good intentions on the part of the interfering family member (usually the parent), but somehow the message or desires get muddled, and those good intentions lead to avoidable human errors.

At the root of some of these generation conflicts lies sexual jealousy—the desire of the child for the parent of the opposite sex, and vice versa. Sexual jealousy is made quite explicit on some of the less traditional soaps. For example, Johnny Ryan (*Ryan's Hope*) has been know to fly into a rage over daughter Mary's sexual involvement with Jack Fenelli (whom she has since married). At one point father says to daughter in effect: I don't want you staying at his apartment and I don't want you in his bed. After this, and much other explicit conversation, Johnny and Jack actually come to blows. Similar emotional tendencies are revealed in *Another World,* a show that is unusually rich in Freudian motifs. Marianne "catches" her mother in the arms of a lover; she clings to her father, all but giving up her social life to be with him. On the same show we find Iris, a middle-aged socialite who is attached to Daddy in her own rather startling ways. "What she really wants is to go to bed with her father," says head writer Harding LeMay. "We come out pretty strongly with that once in a while." Indeed, incestual desires seem to be Iris's specialty. About her marriage, Iris says, "I married Robert because I had to prove to Daddy that I could manage without him." When it turns out that she can't (Robert is one of a series of failed relationships with men) Iris wails that her husband has abandoned her "just like Daddy." She accuses Daddy's younger second wife of "poisoning Daddy's mind against me," whereas it is Iris who is attempting to undermine her father's marriage in every way she

can. Many conflicts result from this troubled behavior. For long periods of time Iris is barred from her father's house—where she nevertheless appears, armed with devious excuses and dressed to the hilt.

In many storylines, mother and daughter compete quite naturally for Daddy's allegiance. Sometimes, however, they compete for the sexual love of some other man. A triangle involving mother and daughter is one of the juicier possibilities open to the scriptwriter. Julie (*Days of Our Lives*) has spent a large part of her romantic energies on a man who belonged to her mother. And Meg and daughter Cal (*Love of Life*) have both had an affair with Rick Latimer. (In both cases, the daughter ultimately gets the man.) Although such arrangements certainly lead to generation conflict, it is not clear that they are meant as comments, psychological or otherwise, on the relationship between generations. They are storylines—and good ones.

The tangled threads of parent-child relationships. Cal Latimer (*Love of Life*) now married to her mother's ex-boyfriend, retains a warm daughter-like closeness to her mother's ex-husband, Eddie. Cathy Craig (*One Life to Live*) has been a drug user and an unwed mother, but her long-suffering father continues to offer her support and affection. Scheming irresponsible Molly (*Another World*) resents her mother Emma's old-fashioned strictness and her interference.

Misplaced and mistaken parentage is another problem that may say more about the soaps than it does about actual generation conflict. A fair number of children discover in young adulthood that their parentage is not as they suppose, and that they have a new parent waiting in the wings. This is primarily a story device, and secondarily a reflection of those fantasies many of us have upon reaching adolescence. But it does complicate relationships. When the child discovers his 'real' or new parent, he accuses his 'psychological' parent of lies and deception. Children who have felt called upon to make such accusations include Mike, Trish, and Brooke (*Days of Our Lives*), Phil Brent (*All My Children*), and Laurie (*Young and Restless*). Typically the child embarks upon a search for the "truth," in which the psychological parent is seen as an opponent. The psychological parent is not usually rejected—just morally challenged.

In addition to providing bizarre family images, the soaps show

In the soaps, a child's psychological parent is often not his natural parent. Holly Bauer (*Guiding Light*) is trying to fill the gap left in nephew Freddie's life by his mother's death. Laurie (*The Edge of Night*) was raised by her natural father and his wife--who is not her mother.

parents and children as we know them to be. We find mothers like Jennifer counseling their daughters against unwise premarital sex (*Young and Restless*). We find mothers like Ada advising their daughters not to neglect their husbands for the sake of their careers (*Another World*). And we hear countless mothers telling daughters and sons to come to their senses. (It's usually phrased, "I only hope you come to your senses," and it usually means, "I only hope you work things out," which means, "stay married!") Sometimes parents are used to point out snobbery and other socially destructive attitudes. (For example, mothers object to their sons' marrying girls of poor "background" or to their daughters' dating denim-clad art students.)

The soaps seem to be especially rich in those motherly comments to which none of us listens in real life: "The last thing you need to worry about is clothes—what you need is a job," says long-suffering Mona to Erica (*All My Children*). Or "You can't pick up after yourself—How're y'gonna work?" (Emma to Molly, *Another World*). The soap mother can be supportive in times of trouble, and deadly in times of romance, but she has little effect as a nag. Alma (*As the World Turns*) expresses it best when she says that she doesn't know what to say to daughter Lisa: "It just makes her mad if I tell her she's done the right thing, and it makes her even madder to hear that she's done the wrong thing!" All very normal.

Parent-child relationships in the soaps are normal in yet another way; they grow and change. Families age. Sometimes, it's true, they age in peculiar ways. (Children who grow from five to nine years of age over the weekend will have the opportunity to become parents more quickly than most of us.) Still, the soaps show us a natural process whereby children become teenagers, parents, and grandparents. The longevity of some programs is such that generation developments will be mirrored in the viewer's own experience. One woman began a letter to *As the World Turns* by

More adoptions. Ruth Martin (*All My Children*) adopted and raised her nephew Phil, and they are very close. Jo (*Search For Tomorrow*) has also won the warm affection of her adopted son, Bruce.

noting that "my son was born the same time as Tom Hughes was," and it is not unusual for college students to mark the beginning of a personal involvement by remembering which of their favorite characters had a baby, or got married at that time. No other popular form follows families so intently, except for the multi-volume "family saga" (and since we can read this all at once, if we wish, it seldom keeps us company over all the days of our lives).

Portrayal of generations and generation conflict does change over the years. It is only lately, for example, that parents and children have been able to argue about sexual "lifestyles." It is only within the last decade that the divorcing parent has become so common a problem to young adult children. Each generation differs in its needs and expectations and the soaps, reflecting real life, pick this up. The soap opera will continue to have material for generation conflicts. Franny Hughes will slowly turn into a grandmother. Little Philip Tyler may be expected to embark upon the difficult path of fatherhood himself. And problems—usual and unusual—will appear.

"RELEVANT" ISSUES

10

The soaps have always been popular because they tell stories—because they entertain. A good soap is, traditionally, the one that makes you tune in tomorrow, no matter what your previous plans. In recent years, however, soaps have been judged and received on a different basis. How *relevant* is this soap? asks the serious viewer (who's not sure he's a "fan"). What is it teaching our young people? asks the mother (who enjoys them anyhow).

The concern with relevancy in the soaps is perhaps inevitable. Any form of entertainment that reaches 20 million people daily will be influential—so why not for the public good? "I sincerely believe that these various programs influence society in a tremendous way," writes a viewer from Michigan, "...the writers and producers of ABC, NBC, CBS have a great responsibility in their future endeavors, since they can play a big hand in reshaping sociological attitudes of the mass media." Many share her view.

There is, moreover, a natural respect for the story as social comment. When Executive Producer John Conboy pointed out that a rape story on *The Young and the Restless* had a more profound effect on the public than did several serious documentaries, he was only proving the point. We care what happens to people like Chris Brooks much more than we care what happens to people-in-general. Although writers and producers must put story first, and social comment second, this leaves plenty of opportunities. Dickens, who is routinely compared to the soap writer, was concerned with economic oppression, criminal justice, child abuse, corruption, etc. And his stories were no worse for this, we know.

Today's serial form, the soap opera, deals only minimally with the kind of social issue that interested Dickens. Seldom in the soaps do we encounter the poor or oppressed as a class of people. There are a few struggling lower-middle-class families (the Fosters, *Young and Restless*; the Claytons, *Days of Our Lives*; the Vinnie Woleks, *One Life to Live*); but most of the action is very upper-middle-class. Characters do not suffer from discrimination in employment or criminal justice, or from exploitative landlords, bosses, and politicians. (Or, if they do, it's not because they're poor.) Only in

113

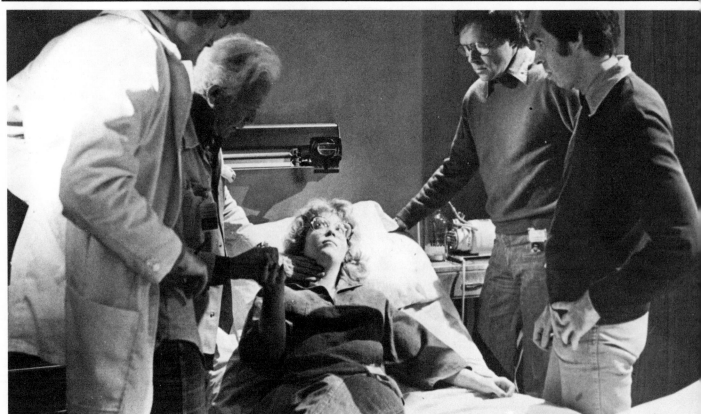

Drug abuse

When Cathy Craig, fourth from right, attended drug therapy sessions on *One Life to Live,* real addicts participated in the discussion. The sequence was filmed on location at Odyssey House, a rehabilitation facility in New York City. Viewer response was generally supportive.

Obesity

Although alcoholism and drug abuse appear regularly on the soaps, *The Young and the Restless* is the only show to deal with obesity. Joann Curtzynski began eating as a result of a loss of self-esteem. She had quit school to put her husband through, and this meant taking menial jobs that did not interest her. She started over-eating, and hating herself more and more. Finally husband Jack turned to other women, aggravating Joann's problem. Now, with Brock Reynold's help, Joann is learning to love and trust herself. In the beginning she thought that if she wanted to be happy, she'd have to be slim; but Brock pointed out a perfectly happy fat woman! What's important is how one feels about oneself. Joann's goal is to learn to feel lovable and worthy—and then lose weight. So far it's working.

Another World, Edge of Night, and *Days of Our Lives* are we sometimes made aware of the existence of less fortunate classes, as classes.

The problems of black Americans are not dramatized either. "No black on the programs is either unemployed or on welfare" notes M.L. Ramsdell in *The Family Coordinator.* Small town settings like Oakdale, Rosehill, and Pine Valley simply do not have many blacks—and those who do appear are invincibly middle class. For example, the black characters on *All My Children* include a doctor, nurse, and high-powered social services administrator. Recently featured (but not a regular member of the cast) was a black pimp; however, nobody took him seriously as a black image. (He drew no hate mail from whites or letters from the black community when he first appeared, and no more than 100 letters at the height of the story, according to Producer Bud Kloss.) In case the viewer missed the point, the black pimp was ultimately vanquished by the good black doctor, the representative soap figure.

On daytime, the only black family which is poor and might therefore offer opportunities for the presentation of different social viewpoints, are the Grants (*Days of Our Lives*). Mrs. Grant is a strong, God-fearing woman, married to a reformed alcoholic. She and her husband come across as "real" blacks in that their behavior, beliefs and speech patterns seem to have been affected by the black experience. (They do not appear on the scene as accomplished middle class; nor do their children, though it is clear that ambitions for medicine and law will lead the younger Grants to middle-class professions and lifestyles.) The Grants occasionally comment on poverty and racial discrimination. And they have had their problems with interracial romance. Naturally they draw an outrageous volume of hate mail. Typical is this letter from a woman from Louisiana:

> One of the best soap operas has been *Days of Our Lives.* But now they have brought in that whole black family. A wonderful cast, all so beautiful, polished, and handsome, do not fit in with "black family." The show is very distasteful to me now. I turn to other shows and will not look at a show going too far.

Black people should have their own soap operas, some say. As of now, they don't. And so black viewpoints and black-white relationships are not really a subject on daytime. It's a pity, from the dramatic standpoint. What fine handwringing—and what fine drama—might take place if Nancy Hughes

Prison conditions

This year on *Love of Life,* Ben Harper was convicted of bigamy and sent to prison. At first his imprisonment was marked by boredom and depression; later he learned of the violence that is equally characteristic of prison life. He was subjected to physical attacks, and even to attempted rape. The show tried to realistically depict the cruelty and degradation experienced by men behind bars. (In addition, this story marked the first time that male rape was ever discussed on a daytime serial.)

The "right to die" issue

On *Ryan's Hope,* Dr. Seneca Beaulac was tried for having disconnected the respirator which was keeping his wife alive, in an irreversible state which Seneca defined as death. The trial dealt seriously with legal definitions of death, and the ethical dilemma faced by physicians and relatives. Seneca was convicted, and can no longer practice medicine. He is usefully employed in the administration of the neurology and neurosurgery department at Riverside Hospital. The "right to die" issue has also been raised on *Search for Tomorrow, One Life to Live,* and more recently on *The Doctors* and *The Young and the Restless.*

were confronted with new black neighbors in a changing neighborhood!

Inattention to poverty subcultures and to black Americans may be explained by the fact that the soaps are, and claim to be, a reflection of white middle-class America. But there is more to it than that. The truth is that there is little attention to hard and unpleasant issues even when they affect the middle class. For example, the soaps more or less ignored Viet Nam. In a genre that specializes in poignant confusion, it is strange indeed that Phil Brent (*All My Children*) was the only MIA to return unexpectedly to a long-lost love. In a genre where sudden death is unfortunately common, heroines did not lose sons or husbands in Viet Nam. The war did not even produce one good amnesia victim.

Political corruption is another area largely ignored by the soaps, despite the dramatic potential (blackmail, court-room scenes, sex- and power-play, etc.) There are some exceptions. *Love of Life* did a story involving Jeff Hart which, oddly enough, paralleled Watergate in many respects and hit the air at about the same time (though it was of course formulated earlier). *The Edge of Night* is more generally concerned with corruption, and there is a sense of social commitment on the part of main characters Mike Karr and Adam Drake. Perhaps most interesting is *Ryan's Hope,* which started out with a politically active family at its center. Not too long ago, Frank Ryan was an aspiring politician, and sister Mary and her husband were reporters who specialized in exposé. These characters were dramatically equipped and motivated to deal with problems of political corruption; however they have since given themselves over to custody battles, surprise pregnancies, auto accidents and other personal problems. So far all that has surfaced is a nursing home investigation, which came to an abrupt and inconclusive end, as do so many in real life.

Why the avoidance of "relevant" issues? According to one well-known writer who has worked on both traditional and "relevant" soaps, the networks simply do not like political stories. They prefer love stories because, they say, their viewers do.

For this reason, the soaps are much more successful in treating relevant issues which are incidental to love stories and other personal crises. Rape is one such relevant issue. It is not an uncommon occurrence on *The Young and the Restless.* The show has been praised for giving important information on the reporting of rape; the psychological reactions of the victim; and the

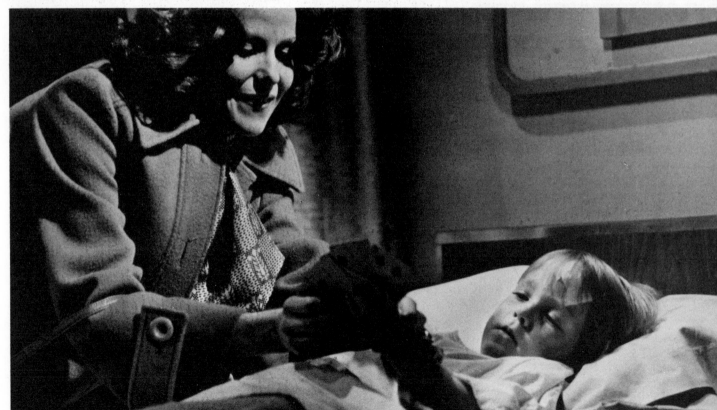

Interracial romance

This past year *Days of Our Lives* began a most controversial and contemporary storyline—interracial romance. It started innocently enough when David Banning, traumatized by life in Salem, ran away. He found a home with the Grants, a poor but proud black family on the other side of the tracks. David became friends with the Grant children, Danny and Valerie. But friendship led to something more when David found himself attracted to Valerie. Everyone in town, including the Grants, was afraid the two would fall in love. Valerie began dating a black medical student, and tried to avoid David as much as possible. But it didn't work. David asked Valerie to marry him and she said yes. Like most young lovers on the soaps, David and Valerie can be expected to experience changes of heart and mind on the way to the altar. In the meantime, the Grants are taking the engagement very hard.

Child abuse

In 1974 *All My Children* took some time to present a storyline on child abuse. Stacy Coles beat her little boy; it was pointed out that many people beat their children, and that help is available. Stacy realized she had a problem, and presto, she and her husband and child were gone. The story was neither fully developed nor integrated with other events in Pine Valley. But it was daring, for daytime.

implications for her family and loved ones. *The Young and the Restless* has even taken up the predicament of the accused rapist, through the character of Ron Becker.

Another personal problem with "relevant" overtones is drug abuse. *One Life to Live* showed Cathy Craig attending a drug treatment group at Odyssey House in New York City. Cathy and other drug users were portrayed as emotionally troubled teenagers and young adults; their hope lay in straightening out their emotional difficulties, in learning to know and express themselves. Mike Powers (*The Doctors*) had similar growing-up problems. In fact, most of the hard drug users on the soaps are confused young people who mature and reform. Interestingly enough, marijuana, the one drug with which many young people have direct experience, is ignored. To date, only one joint has been smoked by the young soap generation.

For older characters, drug abuse means alcoholism. This is one large social problem that looms large on the soaps as well. The course and treatment of the illness varies. But one trend is clear: alcoholics eventually reform or they leave the story. This is all to the good, since viewer identification with the alcoholic appears to be quite strong. One viewer went so far as to admit that she matched Kay Chancellor glass for glass when Kay had a drinking problem (*Young and Restless*); and she stopped drinking right along with Kay!

There is no stereotype alcoholic on the soaps. Most are just people who cannot cope with personal problems. Paul Grant (*Days of Our Lives*) turned to liquor because as a black he encountered many frustrations in his everyday life—poverty, unemployment, family burdens. (This was never shown, as Paul arrived on the story a reformed alcoholic; but his reformation has been discussed and occasionally tested.) Adele Hamilton (also *Days of Our Lives*) turned to drink because the man she loved did not love her; because she had an illegitimate child to raise and little in the way of financial resources, etc. (Adele was at one point shown attending group meetings for alcoholics.) Scott Phillips (*Search for Tomorrow*) turned to drink because of failed marriages. All of the above appeared as sympathetic characters, or "just plain folks." All hurt others, particularly those they loved.

"Bad" characters (that is, characters who normally cause trouble) also drink. Among them are Kay Chancellor (*Young and Restless*), John Dixon and Susan Stewart (*As the World Turns*) and Phoebe Tyler (*All My Children*). Like other alcoholics they drink because of personal problems—but here it's

Teenage alcoholism

Young Lynn Henderson on *Love of Life* uses alcohol to escape her problems, much as adults do. She comes from a troubled home, and is in desperate need of love and security. Motherly Vanessa has taken an interest in Lynn, providing her with a home, and helping her learn to trust herself and others. Lynn is remaining sober for longer and longer periods—though she has not yet solved her problems.

more than an inability to cope. Bad characters tend to be the sole cause of their problems, and the use of alcohol is perhaps incidental. The viewer tends not to be so sympathetic. Of course alcoholics—good *and* bad—feel sorry for themselves. All are destroying their lives and their relationships.

The soaps do not treat alcoholism as a "relevant" issue. That is, they do not (as with drugs) provide social insight or instruction. Alcoholism is presented as the antithesis to real life, the choice people make when they don't know if they want to go on living. Reformation is an affirmation of life. Many alcoholics turn to God in the course of reform, whereas other troubled characters tend to turn to wise old doctors and family members.

Not so prevalent as alcoholism is mental illness, another problem which soaps seldom present in social terms. Although characters sometimes end up (temporarily) in psychiatric hospitals, the soaps do not show the abuse or incompetence that exists therein. An exception is, again, *The Young and the Restless*. When Leslie was confined in a New York institution, viewers were shown the shapeless gowns, the frightened inmates—the whole depressing environment.

In most other instances, mental illness is a way of getting a character off the show for a long or short period. The illness is usually termed a "breakdown" and is therefore thought to be temporary (the result of a particular story development). For example, Eleanor Conrad (*The Doctors*) suffered a breakdown (never shown on screen) because she was unable to cope with having a baby; Erica Brent (*All My Children*) was unable to cope with having a miscarriage. Faith Coleridge (*Ryan's Hope*) broke down when a psychotic kidnapped and killed her much-loved father. Leslie Brooks (*Young and Restless*) fell apart as a result of fantastic love and career pressures. When such temporary difficulties are resolved, the patient recovers. Chronic illnesses like schizophrenia, autism, and manic depressive disorder are almost never dealt with. There have been a few cases of what appears to be multiple personality reaction (Victoria Lord, *One Life to Live*; Serena Farraday, *Edge of Night*) but these are played for story value, with little attention to the psychiatric problem or society's treatment of it. Similarly, "psychotics" appear from time to time as storyline devices; they kill, kidnap, and threaten people.

In addition to "breakdowns" and storyline psychotics, the soaps deal with what might be termed "adjustment problems." On *The Young and the Restless*, characters contend with obesity and mastectomy. On *All My Children,* a mother learns to accept retardation in her newborn child. On *Love of Life* and *Days of Our Lives*, characters frankly discuss problems of frigidity and impotence. Homosexuality (in the form of a real homosexual character) has not yet appeared on the soaps, though a number of shows have reportedly considered storylines that deal more or less explicitly with homosexual orientations. Not only is this a subject presumably distasteful to a large portion of the American public; it is also difficult to show the motivation, given the conventions of daytime TV. It's "not good story."

Generally speaking, creators and producers will deal with a socially relevant topic only if they feel they can do so without compromising the story and its characters. They want to tell stories that "come out of people," not out of the news. Producers like Joe Willmore (*As the World Turns*) are careful to point out that they mean to entertain, and "not to preach." Writers are not much more adventuresome. They can't afford to be, if they want to hold their audience.

Agnes Nixon (*All My Children*) admits that she likes to do "a public service thing" every once in a while. But this, she says, takes careful study, and sometimes more understanding than currently exists. For example, one can't present an informative homosexual story in the absence of a psychiatric definition of homosexuality. Nor can one construct a satisfying story if the audience is politically divided in its reactions toward a character. Will the homosexual character "work" as a hero? Will the interracial couple come across as typically star-crossed? It's hard to tell.

Few writers would claim that their soaps are socially "relevant" or "redeeming." They make a more modest and attractive claim. The soaps are educational; they show us how people deal with their problems. When Harding LeMay (*Another World*) shows us a social worker in action, he calls it a "peripherally educational thing." When Agnes Nixon does an episode on uterine cancer, she (and the American Cancer Society) call it a public service. In any case the relevant educational message comes out of the story and its characters. Story—not message—is the rationale behind the soaps. Story may involve a coffee table confrontation between two troubled housewives; or it may involve an enlightening visit from a social worker. But it seldom involves controversial commitments or political stands. The networks don't want it, and neither does Peoria.

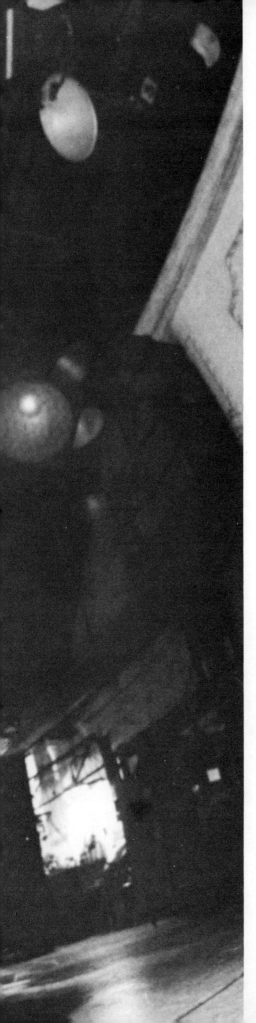

MAKING A SOAP

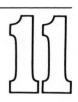
"It's like an under-rehearsed opening night every day," is how actor Stefan Schnabel (Dr. Stephen Jackson, *Guiding Light*) describes the making of a soap. "The funny thing is, practically everybody feels that way....every day, every time you do it."

It's no wonder. The soap actor's day begins at about 7:30 a.m. and ends in mid-afternoon with what is the first and the only performance—the "opening night"—of a complicated drama. The amount of creative and technical talent that is needed to produce each day's show is truly staggering.What begins as an entry in the Head Writer's "bible," must be worked out in story and production conferences, dialogued, directed, taped, and finally aired some six months after the initial conception.

For all the people behind the scenes—the directors, production assistants, costume designers, musicians, technical directors, and many others—the schedule is difficult and exhilarating. For the actors and actresses, it is nothing short of remarkable. "Actors must learn their lines quickly and be ready to adjust to last-minute script changes," says a CBS Casting Director, "They must know immediately what the director wants in their portrayal of a particular character. If something changes suddenly on camera, an actor must be able to cover up smoothly, so as not to interrupt the flow of the plot...." There is little retaping in soap opera. There isn't time for it, and generally it isn't necessary.

The people who make the soap know exactly how to turn the seven hours of every working day into the twenty-two minutes and thirteen seconds of drama we see on a half-hour show. And, if this isn't accomplishment enough, the hour-long shows are on double shift and doing just as well. The making of a soap is one of the most efficient operations going. Everyone from cameraman to Executive Producer is totally committed to quality drama within budget and on time.

The soap actor delivers his lines before a camera like that above. The production process is videotape. It does not require of the actor great projection or larger-than-life gestures (as theater sometimes does). In fact, actors speak in normal voice tones, and move naturally within small room-like settings. Were it not for the ever-present camera, one could not easily distinguish the soap scene from real life.

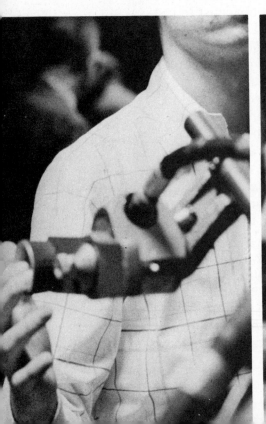

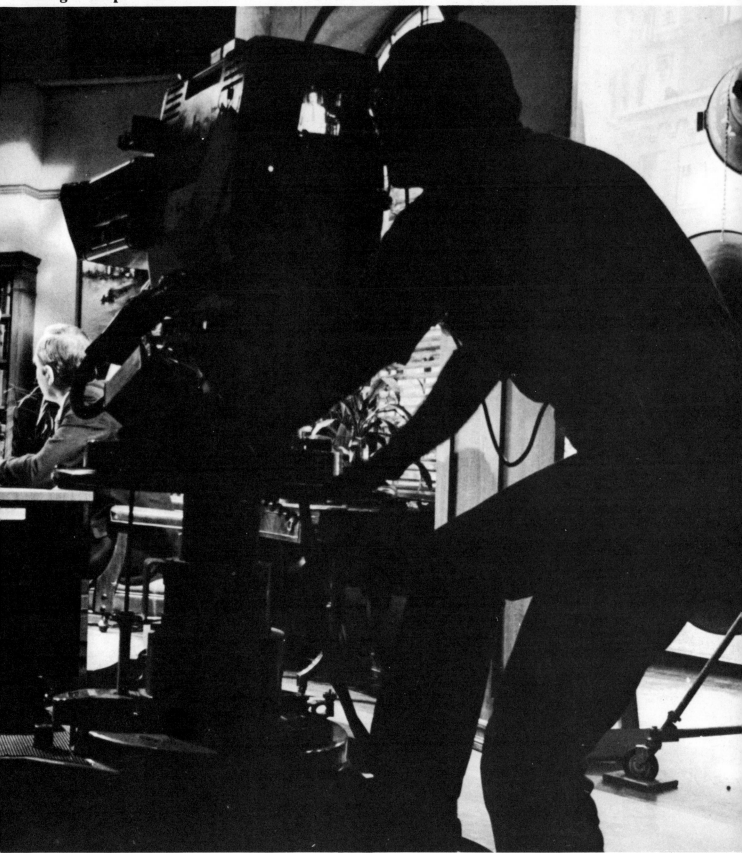

Above, the camera moves in on John Gabriel (Seneca Beaulac) during a confrontation scene on *Ryan's Hope*. The show is located in a relatively small studio on 53rd Street in New York.

Making a Soap: Lighting and Sound

Where there are cameras, there are lights and action. At left, a technician (or "gaffer") re-positions a klieg light, in response to a request from the lighting director. The scene is the kitchen of "Ryan's." Below is the light grid—an overhead view of the many light fixtures that may be brought into play during a taping. Here, we are looking down on *Another World*.

Camera and lights—the visual—are all of
the picture, but only half of the taping.
Sound must be balanced with image.
Above is the monitor for the sound man,
which, in this case, is a sound woman. The
actor who appears on the monitor is
Daren Kelly (Danny Kennicott) of *All My
Children*. Another sound woman from
this set is shown below on the mike boom.
An unusual number of technicians on *All
My Children* are women.

On the set, the actors are only partly conscious of the
camera and overhanging mike boom. At left is a run-
through of a scene between C. David Colson (Tom Hughes)
and Dennis Cooney (Jay Stallings) of *As the World Turns*.

Above is one of the large CBS studios that houses *As the World Turns*. Within each alcove is a set—kitchen, livingroom, office, etc. Not all shows have semi-permanent or standing sets, as does *As the World Turns*. When space is at a premium, sets are removed and reconstructed, day by day, as needed. Occasionally, space must be made for an automobile, a boat, or some other large object (left). The stage manager (right) positions props and performers prior to run-through. Nancy Addison (Jill Coleridge) awaits the signal to move through the swinging door which leads to "Ryan's" kitchen.

Making a Soap: The Set as a Workplace

Below are some of the on-set devices which are consulted by actors, directors, and technicians. At left is a studio monitor, one of several on the floor. Kelly Wood (Mary Ellison) is comforted by a neighbor during this run-through of *As the World Turns.*

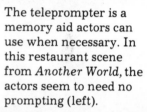

The teleprompter is a memory aid actors can use when necessary. In this restaurant scene from *Another World,* the actors seem to need no prompting (left).

At right is the slate, TV's equivalent to the movie's clapboard. "V.T.R." stands for video tape recorder. Below, we see a cue card held before Frank Telfer (Lew Dancy), Julia Duffy (Penny Dancy), and Jonathan Hogan (Jerry Dancy). The cue card is worked by hand and used in conjunction with the teleprompter.

Another World has standing sets, but some reconstruction goes on nonetheless, for example, in Iris's livingroom (above). It's enough to tire a fellow out.

Making a Soap: Reading Through

The first step for actors and directors is the early morning rehearsal or "read-through." This usually takes place in a room that resembles a gymnasium. The time here is 8:05; the place is the rehearsal hall at the 57th Street studios of CBS in New York. The show is *As the World Turns,* and the director for this day is John Litvak. Here, he works with Rita McLaughlin (Carol Stallings), Kathryn Hays (Kim Dixon), C. David Colson (Tom Hughes) and Dennis Cooney (Jay Stallings). Scripts are amended where necessary, scenes are interpreted and timed, and many many jokes are cracked. Rita McLaughlin is already in costume, but other members of the cast are in street clothes. Because *As the World Turns* is a two-part or hour-long show, a second read-through, involving different cast members will begin in the early afternoon, in preparation for the day's second taping.

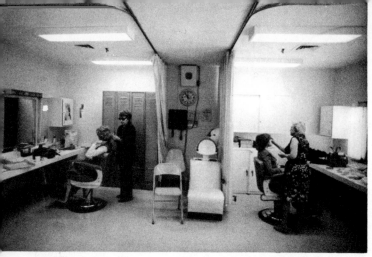

"Make-up" is the room where actresses and actors are made up and coiffured before dress rehearsal. If the read-through begins at 8:00, and blocking on the set proceeds normally, "make-up" takes place around noon. Above is "make-up" at *As the World Turns*. The make-up artist (also seen with C. David Colson, far right) has been with the show since its beginning more than twenty years ago. In addition to beautifying, she is adept at "aging" characters. As for the amount of make-up, she tends to go along with the actress's preference, generally using more make-up on younger and overtly glamorous types. The hair-styling on *As the World Turns* is affectionately termed "Americana." It looks good on Marie Masters (Susan Stewart), right. Below is a comparable "make-up" operation at *Another World*. The Director and production assistant, at rear, chat with performers during the make-up break.

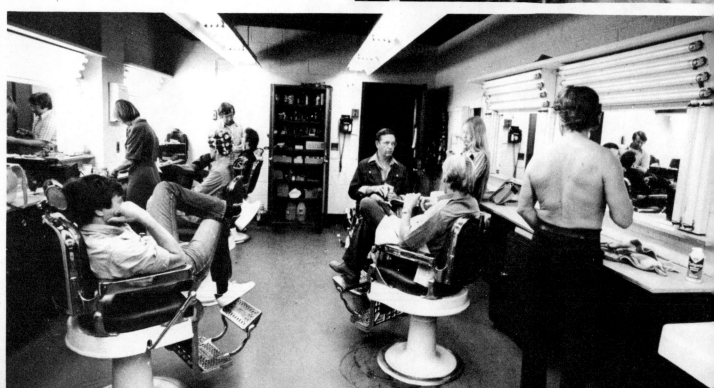

Making a Soap: Making Up

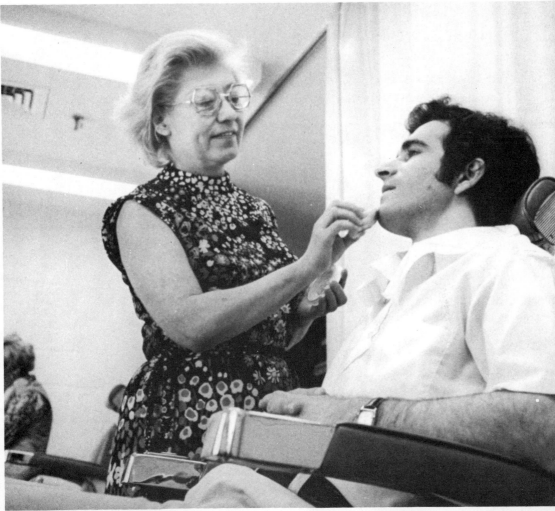

Even on the set a touch-up can be had whenever necessary. At right, seated before a lighted mirror at the back of the studio, is Marie Masters.

Making a Soap: Directing

In dress rehearsal, and later in the Control Room, the Director determines what "works." He is responsible for pacing, for movement of performers and readiness of technicians, and for overall interpretation of the script. Left, Ira Cirken, Director for *Another World,* confers with Toni Kalem (Angie Perrini), as his production assistant looks on. Lower left, John Litvak, Director for *As the World Turns,* reviews a kitchen scene with Rita McLaughlin (Carol Stallings). Upper right, Gene Lasko, Associate Producer and Director for *The Doctors* breaks for consultation with Julia Duffy and Jonathan Hogan (Penny and Jerry Dancy), and Sally Gracie (Martha Allen).

The Stage Manager assists the Director; he makes certain that cameras are in position, and, during taping, he acts as liaison between the people on the set and the people in the Control Room.

Making a Soap: "Notes"

After dress rehearsal (and sometimes after run-through as well) director and performers break for "notes"—the director's notes, of course. Here, Henry Kaplan, Director for *All My Children*, reviews his notes on the dress rehearsal and points out areas for improvement or change. His gestures are dramatic, his language colorful, but it doesn't keep everybody awake. Alexander Scourby (lower right) was cast as an out-of-work actor. Others present at this note session are Eileen Herlie (Mrs. Lum), Hugh Franklin (Charles Tyler), Peter White (Linc Tyler), Fran Heflin (Mona Kane), Daren Kelly (Danny Kennicott) and Karen Gorney (Tara Brent). At the director's left is the production assistant.

The Control Room is the nerve center, or brain, of the whole soap operation. In the Control Room, the Director receives images from the cameras. He sees how shots are

setting up, and literally "calls the shots." He communicates with cameramen and other technicians through mike and headset ("OK, hold in there," or "Punch it," etc.). At his side, an assistant times the scenes. Though the studio is off-limits during the taping, the Control Room is relatively free and accessible. Costume and set designers, off-stage actors, and visitors wander through, or stand and watch the taping in progress. (They can also see silent images from competing shows which happen to be airing at the same time.)

Making a Soap: In the Control Room

Above are scenes from the Control Rooms at *Another World* and *The Doctors*: left, from *As the World Turns*.

Making a Soap: Producers

Behind the behind-the-scenes are the Producers (executive and associate). The Producer has overall creative control of the show. He is responsible for everything from the casting decisions to the quality of the lighting. In fact, everything that you see on a soap opera is the result of something the Producer has done or asked somebody else to do. The Producer answers to the owner of the show (network, sponsor, etc.), or to the advertising agency assigned by the owner. He is responsible for working within the philosophy *and* within the budget that have been established. The Producer appears on the set from time to time. For example, John Conboy of *The Young and the Restless* attends most run-throughs, and works with the actors through the director and in conference (upper left). Other times, he's behind the desk conferring over telephone with Head Writer Bill Bell, who lives in Chicago. Conboy's philosophy, framed on the wall behind him, is a quote from Noel Coward that tells him in effect that he can do anything to his public as long as he's not boring. Other Producers shown here are Leslie Kwartin Producer of *Guiding Light* (above); Budd Kloss, Producer of *All My Children* (right); and Paul Rauch, Executive Producer of *Another World* and the new soap *Lovers and Friends* (below).

FANS AND CRITICS

12

In the fall of 1971, *Life* Magazine cited a Harris Poll which should have assured us the soap opera posed no threat to our aesthetic morale. Only 26% of the country was willing to say that they considered "soap operas" as shows "meant for me." *Only* 26%, said *Life*, with a one-word sigh of relief.

The strange thing is that *Life* has since vanished, while *Love of Life* (among thirteen others) continues. It turns out that "only 26%" represented two and a half times the circulation of *Life*—and nothing to sneer about.

Over the years, critics have tried to belittle the soap opera. Or, worse yet, they have ignored it. Whereas a new prime time show will be reviewed by dozens of critics, a soap can run for twenty years with only the barest of critical attention. What attention it does receive will be (except in the fan publications) negative, cutesy, and smug. This seems as true today as it was thirty years ago.

In the earlier days of the radio soap, there was only sporadic sniping in the press, and occasional public frowns from clergymen and women's organizations. Listening to soaps seemed at first a negligible vice. It wasn't until 1942, when there were some sixty fifteen-minute serials on the airwaves, that the first celebrated attack on soaps was published. The attack was launched not by a media analyst, but by a doctor, Dr. Louis I. Berg. In a pamphlet published at his own expense, the doctor heaped indignation on serial drama and offered "scientific" warnings to fans. Berg, after examining a number of women patients, explained that soaps were dangerous to the mental and physical health of American women: "Pandering to perversity and playing out destructive conflicts, these serials furnish the same release for the emotionally distorted that [was] supplied to those....who in the unregretted past, cried out in ecstasy at a witch burning." He added that soaps were capable of causing a wide range of ailments from tachycardia (rapid heartbeat) to gastro-intestinal disorders! Thirty years later, we might consider Dr. Berg a

Stars of *One Life To Live* Jennifer Harman, who plays Cathy Craig Lord, and George Reinholt, who plays her husband Tony, meet some of their fans. Actress Teri Keane (upper far right) plays Naomi Vernon on this popular soap.

crackpot or a put-on. In his own time, however, he was taken very seriously. His claims caused controversy and considerable network discomfort. Both CBS and NBC conducted research studies to determine the truth of the doctor's pronouncements.

Needless to say, Dr. Berg and his pamphlet passed into historical oblivion. But soon after, a far more effective critic took on the soap opera. He was one of America's greatest humorists, James Thurber. In a five-part series in the *New Yorker* in the spring and summer of 1948, Thurber dissected serials with his usual razor-sharp wit. His essays, though directed at radio soaps, are funny (and still applicable) today.

Thurber's articles set a tone that has proven almost irresistible to later critics. In addition to witty

turns of phrase, he was able to sustain an overall quality that combined bemused wonder, sardonic understanding, and a trace of exhaustion. For example, at one point, he borrowed the convoluted tone of soap opera itself. Mocking both the improbability of serial plots and the refrain of the inevitable narrator, he wrote, "Can a beautiful young stepmother, can a widow with two children, can a restless woman married to a preoccupied doctor, can a mountain girl in love with a millionaire, can a woman married to a hopeless cripple, can a girl who married an amnesia case—can they find happiness and the good soap opera way of life?" The same mock refrain has appeared in many other soap articles despite the fact that narrators went out of fashion years ago.

For comic effect Thurber would crowd a month of plot into one paragraph—a technique repeatedly used by later writers as well. A review of *Ryan's Hope,* in the Washington *Post,* reads like vintage Thurber: "Frank's lively young brother Pat is an intern at Riverside Hospital, where he is the confidant of shy young Dr. Bucky Carter, who has a hopeless crush on dedicated young Dr. Faith Coleridge, who is obviously overly devoted to her widower father Dr. Ed Coleridge, chief of neurology and neurosurgery..." Streams of accidental pregnancies, hopeless love affairs, amnesia cases, etc., are reported by the critics in breathless sentences. In such concentrated forms soap opera stories are usually funny—and writers make the most of this.

In fact, when it comes to soaps, critics seem to have a compulsion to be funny. Perhaps the principal reason is the lack of humor in the shows themselves. As writers accurately point out, soaps seldom laugh at themselves or at life. Jokes are told once every ten years, if at all, on the traditional soaps—a point that drives some critics to distraction. Soaps are in fact so unfunny that a critic can either rise above them and laugh once in a while, or become as deadly serious as the material.

But whatever the reason, most critics do try to be funny—not only those who hate soaps but also those who like them. To gain a few points from readers, even a semi-serious piece of criticism will have a joke or two, usually in the form of clever similes and puns. Critics report that men "all" look

like, 1) "Gore Vidal," (*Newsweek*), or 2) "up-and-coming Madison Avenue execs," (*New Republic*). They tell us that a plot was "aborted" or that a pause was "pregnant." One writer concluded an article on a medical note, dryly saying that the loose plot ends needed to be "sutured up."

While the critics like to pun, they have a long way to go to match headline writers. Soap, suds, washing, detergents, are continually played on: "Massive Detergence," (*The Reporter*), "The Suds of Time March On," (*Redbook*), "The New Soap Operas—They Still Don't Wash," (The New York *Times*),"the Wring Cycle," (*Reader's Digest*), and so on. These headlines may be clever but they tell us little about the tone or content of the articles. The four critical articles cited are actually quite different in most respects—except, of course, in their punning titles.

Puns and one-liners are mere frills in much of the writing on soap opera. Writers invariably aim for the humorous tone, and in the process, some fall into an attitude that is more a pose than a literary style. They are, they say, worn down by daytime drama. At least one critic wrote as if he were in a semi-daze, as though the strain of watching had disconnected his brain synapses. In an article entitled, "What am I doing watching this sordid mess?" TV critic Charles Sopkin describes his week of soap watching as a time of amazement and confusion. He intimated that following the plot complications and characters was as difficult (and required the same kind of analytic skill) as doing complex math problems.

Lee Patterson, who plays Joe Riley on *One Life To Live*, talks to fans at a gathering, and poses for snapshots by some of his admirers.

Other critics adopt a pose of sophisticated drollery, setting themselves above soap opera experience. Writing in the Montreal *Star* a few years ago, Paul McKenna Davis "bemoaned" the cancellation of "Peyton Place" because he would no longer be able to *not* watch it. He explained that he'd only seen it in the first place because his glasses had been broken—keeping him from reading a book by Lionel Trilling—and he had had the choice on television of "Peyton Place," a political speech, or "a typical CBS documentary about how to milk a water buffalo."

Many critics, though they never say so, appear to be a little uncomfortable writing about soaps at all. Perhaps this is due to the misconception that still persists—that all critics loathe serials. Though it's not true and probably never was, critics repeat the charge from time to time and then go on to write articles that sound almost apologetic. "Consider the lowly soap opera," one critic wrote. Said another, "Starting at the witching wedding hour of high noon, the soggy procession of soap operatic repertoire begins." Both those articles were favorable, written by fans. It seems that in print even champions of the genre feel the need to make a few wisecracks about it.

Though most soap opera writing is light, it is not always frivolous, and there have been times when critics have entirely swallowed their giddy prose, unarched their brows, and have written serious statements on the subject. Some well-known people have dismissed soaps with an imperious thumbs

Jeffrey Pomerantz (above) greets his public; stars Val Dufour (near right above), Jacquie Courtney (near right below) and Michael Storm (far right) obligingly sign autographs.

down. (David Susskind, for example, said, "Soaps are beneath intelligent notice.") But such ivory tower pronouncements, which avoid reality and add nothing to our understanding of serial drama, are opinions rather than serious criticism. The latter begins with a willingness on the part of the critic to acknowledge an artistic or social context in soap opera. Few critics are willing to do that; but from the time of the hysterical Dr. Berg, some have.

Among them, the former New York *Times* film critic, Renata Adler, stands out. In the same *New Yorker* where Thurber once pilloried radio soaps, Adler wrote thoughtfully and analytically, as both a fan and critic. She answered the punsters and the ivory tower critics firmly. "Serial drama is no joke… There does not seem to be a single sense in which soap opera can be construed as an escapist form."

Also she explained what, in her opinion, is the essence of the genre. "Soaps simply bring things home…And what they bring home is the most steady, openended sadness to be found outside life itself." Her article is surely the most resounding defense of serial dramas. She even defended the entangled plots and the melodramatic writing. "Perhaps the grand oral tradition rambled on this way, and then we had the *Iliad* and the *Nibelungenlied.*" A far cry from Thurber, who wondered how serial script writers could keep their sanity turning out what he called a "Niagara of prose."

Adler's article is unique. Other critics tend to focus less on the literary content of soaps and more on the social ramifications. Author Marya Mannes took on television serials in the now defunct

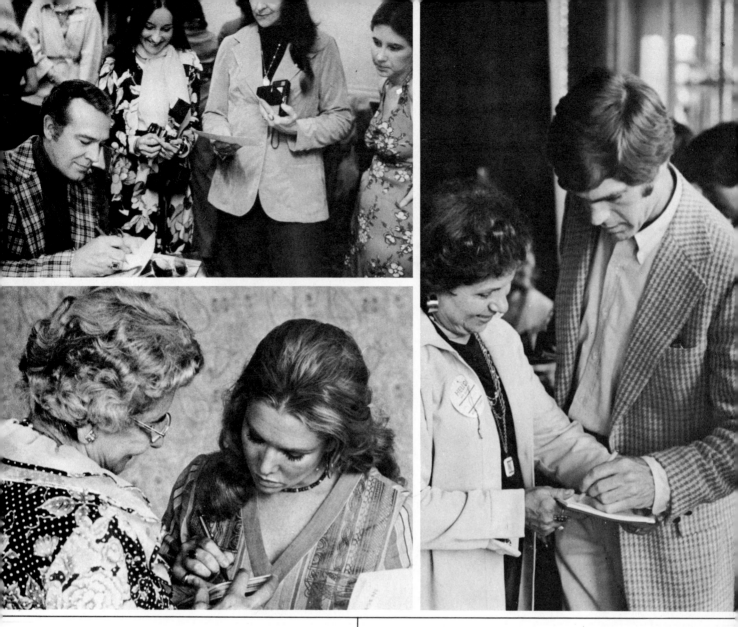

Reporter magazine in 1961. While she found fault with soaps as entertainment, she damned them mainly because she felt they were brainwashing American women. Soaps, she said, feed their audience an unreal stereotyped world and portray it as achievable reality, all for the purpose of encouraging women to buy the sponsor's product. Mannes went on to say that soap operas represented, "the daily confirmation, as normal and desirable, of flabbiness as the human condition: sentimentality, lack of control or discipline, fuzziness of thinking and the couch-inspired philosophy that bad people...are more to be pited than censured..."

Though soaps have since changed in many respects, other critics have periodically repeated and elaborated Mannes' charges. A writer for *Family Coordinator* claimed that sponsors were selling a lifestyle that placed a premium value on middle-class consumption. Families were all of a type—a type that viewers were urged to emulate. Yet that type was unrealistic and the standard perhaps unfair. The author especially described as unfair the portrayal of women, complaining that "real women" were always homemakers and that career-oriented women were treated unsympathetically.

The last charge continues to be debated. Though all critics acknowledge that there is a goodly number of working women in soaps, some regard this as insignificant. Women work as a way to get a man—just a variation on an old theme. Untrue, say soap defenders. More than one soap has been called feminist, and a writer in *Ms.* Magazine stated flatly that she likes soaps "because they are about women." And that seems to include women doctors,

There is no such thing as a typical fan, as a good look at these faces proves. All they have in common is a boundless enthusiasm for "their" show.

women lawyers, and an occasional woman judge.

Part of the critic's problem is that the soaps are not alike. One's impressions of women's roles (or any other issue) depends to some extent on which soaps one is talking about. Unfortunately for criticism, the genre is usually described as though all shows were identical, when, as any fan knows, there are differences in tone and content. Although one soap is not necessarily a guide to any other, some critics watch one, two, or even six soaps and then make pronouncements on serial drama as a whole. While a few critics over the years have praised one soap over another, mixed reviews have become common only in the 1970s. Appraisals have become more balanced.

In determining which soaps are best, critics look primarily for two things: realism and boldness. Serials that are in the traditional (and still very

popular) mold of *As the World Turns* are downgraded in favor of those programs that handle sex, drugs, politics, etc., in a forthright manner. Anthony Astrachan in the *New York Times Magazine* argues that, "Some of the improvement in daytime drama has no doubt been caused by an infusion of realism. It must be easier to write and act well when some of the more ridiculous contortions of classical soap opera are eliminated. Certainly *As the World Turns*, the least realistic of all soaps, is also the worst theater on the air despite the presence of genuine acting talents...Their abilities cannot overcome the show's lethal combination of woodenness and melodrama."

"Realism," "social relevance," "daring," are terms that are creeping into the prose of many present-day soap opera critics. But even as the

television writers have begun to offer a few words of praise, a new group of critics seems to be emerging. Psychologists and social scientists have started writing on soaps and they are not very fond of them (though they seldom wisecrack). Realism, television critics say? Dr. Theodore Rubin in *Ladies Home Journal* answered. "Soap operas are, at best, a pale imitation of life and literature...watched to excess, they can remove us from the centers of our real lives." When this happens, says Dr. Rubin, we no longer need to "fantasize, create, think, relate to other people, or be at all sociable."

Even more damning is an article in *Human Behavior.* It advances the proposition that the unrealistic portrayal of home life is potentially damaging to children. "Every child in the country is affected by soaps. No child can escape the cultural

environment we make and share with each other." And what part do soaps play in that environment? "They do violence to images of family commitment ....by their visual code denying that children are important to family living." Children, the author continued, are unwanted and "disposable," and "nobody really cares." The message of the article is clear: soaps can be harmful psychologically to America's young. (And they used to be harmful only to middle-aged ladies!)

Critics can offer all the warnings they like, but in the end it really doesn't matter what they say. Unlike films, plays, and books, soaps are not affected by the critic's judgment, and the situation is likely to remain that way. Thurber, besides being funny, understood that basic truth. "The audience," he wrote, "has taken control of the daytime serial."

WHO'S WHO OF CHARACTERS AND ACTORS

13

ALL MY CHILDREN

Dr. Charles Tyler *(Hugh Franklin):* a good doctor, good man, and patriarch of the Tyler family; estranged husband to Phoebe; father to Linc and Anne; grandfather to Chuck Tyler. He is romantically committed to secretary Mona Kane.

Phoebe Tyler *(Ruth Warrick):* estranged wife to Charles; mother to Linc and Anne; "grandmother" to Chuck; a ridiculously arrogant woman; a schemer. She believes her family to be far superior to anyone else's.

Lincoln ("Linc") Tyler *(Peter White):* the good and upstanding lawyer in town; husband to Kitty; son to Phoebe and Charles; brother to Anne. He feels very protective toward his new bride and will do anything to make her happy.

Kitty Carpenter Tyler *(Francesca James):* wife to Lincoln Tyler; emotionally, at least, "daughter" to Mrs. Lum (alias "Lucy Carpenter"). She's been transformed from a neurotic girl to a sane and sensible young woman who is trying to better herself; still, a romantic innocent, always vulnerable.

Dr. Chuck Tyler *(Richard Van Vleet):* a good young doctor; grandson to Charles (only); ex-husband to Tara and psychological father to little Phil. He is an idealist with strong feelings of responsibility toward others (some of whom tend to take advantage of his good nature).

Kate Martin *(Kay Campbell):* the matriarch of the Martin family; a widow; mother to Joe and Paul; grandmother to Tara, Tad, and Elizabeth; great-grandmother to little Phil; a warm, understanding and generally non-interfering woman.

Paul Martin *(William Mooney):* a good lawyer; husband to Anne; father to newborn Elizabeth; son to Kate; a family man who tries hard to handle the problems. He and Anne have a "true love."

Anne Tyler Martin *(Judith Barcroft):* wife to Paul Martin; mother to newborn Elizabeth; daughter to Phoebe and Charles; sister to Linc; a young woman of strong faith and stronger emotions. With the birth of her retarded daughter, she is becoming increasingly irrational.

Dr. Joe Martin *(Ray McConnell):* husband to Ruth; father to Tara and grandfather to little Phil; adoptive father to Tad; son to Kate; brother to Paul. He is a complicated and undemonstrative man; a good person, but perhaps too proud.

Nurse Ruth Martin *(Mary Fickett):* wife to Joe; adoptive mother to Phil and Tad; a person of strong family values who has had to come to terms with unexpected emotions, in herself and others.

Dr. Jeff Martin *(Robert Perault):* son to Joe Martin; brother to Tara; a decent, idealistic doctor, much loved by family and friends. He left Pine Valley after the tragic death of his wife Mary—a temporary move, of course.

Tara Martin Brent *(Karen Gorney):* ex-wife to Chuck; and now (finally) wife to Phil; mother to little Phil; sister to Jeff; a good girl, emotionally confused and usually close to tears. She is torn between her "true love" and her son's happiness.

Phil Brent *(Nick Benedict):* husband to Tara; illegitimate son to Nick Davis and Amy (Ruth's long-departed sister), raised by Ruth Martin; Tara's "true love" and natural father to little Phil. Now that he has found his vocation (as a policeman) his main concern is in winning the love and respect of his son.

(Little) Phil Tyler *(Brian Lema):* a small boy with his share of health problems. He is the one person standing in the way of Phil and Tara's happiness (he thinks Chuck is daddy).

Erica Kane Brent *(Susan Lucci):* ex-wife to Phil; daughter to Mona Kane; a delightfully self-centered, scheming, and greedy young woman. She seems to have met her match in Nick Davis—all to the good, since her heart softens too when someone cares.

Mona Kane *(Frances Heflin):* a very good woman; long-suffering mother to Erica; friend, secretary, and romantic interest of Dr. Charles Tyler. As sweet as she is, she can be weak-willed.

Nick Davis *(Lawrence Keith):* a ne'er-do-well who has finally done very well (as owner of "The Chateau" restaurant); natural father to Phil; ex-husband to many; a well-meaning sort, but perhaps a bit worldier than most Pine Valley residents. He is currently involved (if that's the word) with Erica.

Clem Watson *(Reuben Green):* an experienced policeman, working with Phil Brent; a black man, recently divorced.

Dr. Frank Grant *(John Danelle):* a young black doctor; husband to Nancy; good friend to Chuck Tyler and perhaps a little more than that to Caroline. He is a good and earnest man who must come to terms with his wife's independent nature and career.

Nurse Caroline Murray *(Pat Dixon):* Frank Grant's friend, confidante and love interest. She is an idealist, but made of stronger stuff than Frank.

Dr. David Thornton *(Paul Gleason):* a surgeon who temporarily demoted himself to orderly after a painful stint in Viet Nam; an outsider who has experienced much of the world beyond Pine Valley. He is recovering from a disappointment in love, with Ruth Martin. Will he leave town?

Dr. Christina Karras *(Robin Strasser):* a pediatrician; an intelligent and straightforward woman— but strangely haunted by the past.

Danny Kennicott *(Daren Kelly):* a college student, in architecture; brother to the murdered Mary Kennicott Martin; a personable young man who lives in Kate Martin's house.

Brooke English *(Julia Barr):* a college student; niece to Phoebe and currently living with her. She is charming and clever when it comes to getting her own way.

Benny Sago *(Larry Flieschman):* Brooke's hoody boyfriend; a boor, a smart-aleck, and the bane of Phoebe's existence.

Tad Gardner *(Matthew Anton):* an orphan, adopted by Ruth and Joe Martin; a boy about 8 years old who is perceptive, charming and endearing.

Donna Beck *(Candace Earley):* seventeen-year-old prostitute who entered the story when she was admitted to Pine Valley Hospital as a patient; a mixed-up girl from a "bad home," now trying to go right. She is romantically interested in "Doc" Chuck Tyler, her legal guardian.

Mrs. Lum *(Eileen Herlie):* a former carnival performer with a weakness for booze and money (not necessarily in that order). She was hired by Phoebe to impersonate Kitty's mother, Lucy Carpenter, and get Kitty out of town; not a nice woman, but compared to Phoebe a saint.

ANOTHER WORLD

Jim Matthews *(Hugh Marlowe):* a handsome older man; a widower; father to Pat, Russ, and Alice; grandfather to Michael and Marianne, and Sally; brother-in-law to Liz Matthews. He's a kindly,

caring sort with strong moral values; a good advisor to his family.

Liz Matthews *(Irene Dailey):* sister-in-law to Jim

(and romantically interested in him); "Aunt Liz" to practically everyone else. She is a meddlesome type who always means well and always causes trouble.

Alice Matthews Frame *(Susan Harney):* widow of Steven Frame and owner of his business, Frame Enterprises; daughter to Jim; sister to Pat and Russ; adoptive mother to Sally; a good young woman, well-liked by all. She is strong and determined, but sometimes finds it difficult to cope.

Dr. Russ Matthews *(David Bailey):* husband to Sharlene; son to Jim; brother to Pat and Alice; an attractive, but temperamental man.

Sharlene Frame Matthews *(Laurie Heineman):* wife to Russ; sister to Emma Ordway, Willis Frame, and the now-deceased Steven Frame; a good young woman; actually, a country girl who was once a prostitute. She's naive and insecure— and, because of her past, vulnerable.

Pat Randolph *(Beverly Penberthy):* estranged wife to John; mother to Marianne and Michael; daughter to Jim; sister to Russ and Alice; formerly involved with David Gilchrist; a beautiful, believable woman who is rethinking her life in midstream—with some sense of humor.

John Randolph *(Michael M. Ryan):* a lawyer; estranged husband to Pat; father to Marianne and Michael; a complex and intelligent man, at times stubborn and emotional.

Michael Randolph *(Lionel Johnston):* son to Pat and John; twin to Marianne; a headstrong young man; spontaneous, likable, but maybe a little too intense. Surprise—he just married Molly, from the back of our list!

Marianne Randolph *(Ariane Munker);* daughter to Pat and John; twin to Michael; a beautiful young girl who has paid for past mistakes, but will make others. Her parent's break-up created a lot of emotional problems for her.

Darryl Stevens *(Richard Dunne):* a nice college boy who tried to help Marianne solve her problems. He's been romantically involved with Marianne and Molly Ordway.

MacKenzie ("Mac") Cory *(Douglass Watson):* a handsome, wealthy businessman; husband to Rachel; father to Iris Carrington; grandfather to Dennis; and a paternal figure to practically everyone. He's kind, generous, and very good; his only weaknesses are jealousy, and an inability to be alone.

Rachel Cory *(Victoria Wyndham):* a sculptor; wife to Mac; mother to Jamie Frame; stepmother to Iris (who's about her own age); daughter to Ada McGowan. A strong, stubborn, intense and loving woman.

Jamie Frame *(Bobby Doran):* son to Rachel (and the now-deceased Steven Frame); best friend to Dennis Carrington; a good boy. At fifteen (or thereabouts), he is just beginning to notice girls.

Ada McGowan *(Constance Ford):* wife to Gil; mother to Rachel and young Nancy (by different fathers); grandmother to Jamie. She is a hardworking middle-aged housewife with a strong sense of right and wrong.

Gil McGowan *(Dolph Sweet):* a gruff but good-natured policeman; husband to Ada; father to Nancy, and to two sons from a previous marriage; stepfather to Rachel. He is a straightforward, hardworking man who turns to his wife for much of his strength.

Tim McGowan *(not cast):* a newcomer; son to Gil. He fled the country after attempting to steal Frame Enterprises from Steven Frame; but Gil asked Alice to drop the charges and Tim may be on his way back to Bay City soon.

Iris Cory Carrington *(Beverlee McKinsey):* the wealthy and insecure daughter to Mac; mother to Dennis. She's a trouble-maker with an insatiable need for her father's affection; an enemy to Rachel.

Dennis Carrington *(Mike Hammett):* a good boy of about fifteen; son to Iris; grandson to Mac; best friend to Jamie. He has difficulty in coping with his meddlesome mother, particularly when he tries to date a girl "not good enough" for him.

Louise Goddard *(Anne Meacham):* housekeeper for Iris; a kind, gentle woman. She understands Iris's insecurities, and in her own sweet way copes very well; romantically involved with Rocky Olsen.

Rocky Olsen *(John Braden):* Mac and Rachel's stable manager; a thoroughly nice person; romantically involved with Louise.

Ken Palmer *(William Lyman):* a serious artist who conducts art classes for Darryl and Marianne, and gives private lessons to Rachel. He has declared his love to Rachel.

Beatrice Gordon *(Jacqueline Brooks):* mother to Raymond Gordon; grandmother to Sally, Alice Frame's adopted daughter; a good woman who cares too much, worries too much, and is sometimes stifling in her affections. She has left town in order to think over her mistakes, past and present.

Raymond Gordon *(Ted Shackelford):* estranged husband to Olive; son to Beatrice; uncle to Sally; romantically involved with Alice Frame. He will have to acquire a personality—or leave Bay City.

Olive Gordon *(Jennifer Leak):* bitch of a wife to Raymond; a schemer who is both money-hungry and class-conscious. She is interested in John Randolph, her employer.

Sally Frame *(Cathy Greene):* adopted daughter to Alice; grand-daughter to Beatrice; niece to Raymond; about ten years old. She is a very sweet and honest child.

Willis Frame *(Leon Russum):* a once-slick, villainous young man who is learning the error of his ways; brother to Emma and Sharlene and the now-deceased Steven Frame. He has long been the love interest of Angie Perrini—but not until now has he tried to be worthy of her.

Bert Ordway *(Robert Blossom):* husband to Emma; father to Molly.

Emma Ordway *(Tresa Hughes):* wife to Bert; mother to Molly; sister to Sharlene, Willis, and the now-deceased Steven Frame; a farm-town woman with good old-fashioned values.

Molly Ordway Randolph *(Rolanda Mendels):* wife to Michael; daughter to Emma and Bert; niece to Sharlene and Willis; a spoiled young girl who's interested in the good life, and won't let anyone get in her way.

Clarice Hobson *(Gail Brown):* mother to newborn Cory Hobson; a dumb blond with a heart of gold. She is the kind of person everyone wants to protect; currently living with Ada and Gil.

Angela ("Angie") Perrini *(Toni Kalem):* neighbor to Ada and Gil; the traditional Girl Next Door; in love with Willis—but he must prove to her he's really changed.

Dr. David Gilchrist *(David Ackroyd):* an attractive middle-aged doctor; witty and sensitive. He has a history of traumatic short-term relationships with women.

Keith Morrison *(Fred Beir):* a lawyer; friend to Iris, Mac and Rachel; boss to Scott Bradley. He is honest, kind and good—and tries to keep Iris on the straight and narrow.

Dr. Frank Prescott *(Mason Adams):* an older doctor; employer of Liz Matthews.

Brian Bancroft *(Paul Stevens):* a newcomer; chief counsel to Mac Cory.

Scott Bradley *(Michael Goodwin):* lawyer for Mac Cory; handsome, thirtyish.

Jeff Stone *(Dan Hamilton):* an ambitious lawyer without many scruples.

Evan Webster *(Barry Jenner):* a bright and ambitious architect working for Frame Enterprises; currently interested in Angie.

Gwen Parish *(Dorothy Lyman):* an architect who has set her sights on Mac; independent-minded and aggressive, but certainly not malicious.

AS THE WORLD TURNS

Chris Hughes *(Don MacLaughlin):* a lawyer; husband to Nancy; father to Bob, Donald and Penny (who hasn't been seen for years); grandfather to Franny and Tom. He is a very nice sort who usually respects his wife's feelings on family matters.

Nancy Hughes *(Helen Wagner):* matriarch of Oakdale; wife to Chris; mother to Bob, Donald and Penny; grandmother to Tom and Franny. She dispenses faith, hope, and optimism to all—but she can be very stern and uncompromising.

Dr. Bob Hughes *(Don Hastings):* a very good doctor who, after many marriages, is once more a bachelor; son to Chris and Nancy; father to Tom and Franny (by different mothers). He is a kind and loving man, with the usual human flaws.

Donald Hughes *(Martin West):* a lawyer; son to Nancy and Chris; brother to Bob; something of a problem to his family. He isn't really a bad man, but just seems to get involved with the wrong women.

Tom Hughes *(C. David Colson):* a young lawyer; son to Bob Hughes and Lisa Colman; grandson to Chris and Nancy; ex-husband to Natalie Bannon; ex-husband to Carol Stallings (and still in love with her). He is an impulsive young man, moody and romantic.

Natalie Bannon Hughes *(Judith Chapman):* ex-wife to Tom Hughes; an attractive and scheming young woman who's determined to make good and allows nothing to stand in her way.

Franny Hughes *(Maura Gilligan):* daughter to Bob Hughes and the now-deceased Jennifer; niece to Kim Dixon. She's too young to be a real problem— the only thing her elders worry about are babysitters and the fact that she's motherless.

Dr. David Stewart *(Henderson Forsythe):* a good doctor; husband to Ellen; stepfather to Dan; father to Annie and Dawn; grandfather to Betsy and Emmy. He is a staunch supporter and friend to Bob Hughes; a kind and understanding person.

Ellen Stewart *(Patricia Bruder):* wife to David; mother to Dan, Annie, and Dawn; grandmother to Betsy and Emmy; a matriarch with perhaps a bit more tolerance and understanding than Nancy Hughes.

Dr. Dan Stewart *(John Colenback):* a good doctor; husband to Valerie; father to Betsy and Emmy (by different mothers); ex-husband to Susan Stewart; and underneath it all "true love" to Kim Dixon. He's honest, forthright, and intelligent—a solid sort who sometimes lets his emotions get the better of him.

Valerie Conway Stewart *(Judith McConnell):* wife to Dan; ex-sister-in-law to Kim Dixon. She is either a good woman with weaknesses, or a villain with virtues.

Dr. Susan Stewart *(Marie Masters):* ex-wife to Dan; mother to Emmy; a weak woman who has been transformed into a more caring and loving person—the hard way. There is still a strong, selfish streak.

Judge Lowell *(William Johnstone):* grandfather to Ellen Stewart; a kindly old man who is also perceptive and wise (and therefore sought out for advice by his family).

Emmy Stewart *(Jenny Harris):* daughter to Susan and Dan; a lively little girl about six years old. She's caused a few problems for Susan in the past by running away (she now lives with Dan).

Betsy Stewart *(Suzanne Davidson):* a young girl, about twelve, who doesn't know her "uncle Dan" is really her father; an unusually sweet and mature child.

Annie Stewart *(Martina Deignan):* a college student who has decided to become a doctor; daughter to Ellen and David; sister to Dawn and half-sister to Dan.

Dawn ("Dee") Stewart *(Marcia McClain):* youngest daughter to Ellen and David; sister to Annie and half-sister to Dan. Like many college-aged girls, she is somewhat rebellious, somewhat mixed-up, but outgoing and good-natured nonetheless.

Beau Spencer *(Wayne Hudgins):* a young man who is romantically involved with Dee (but who seems to have an eye on Annie as well); a nice boy with problems; the son of wealthy and apparently neglectful parents.

Dr. John Dixon *(Larry Bryggman):* the villainous doctor; ex-husband to Kim and father to her baby; a weak, selfish and sometimes cruel man. He always has ample justification for his misdeeds— even though others can't see it.

Kim Dixon *(Kathryn Hays):* a good, gentle woman who has suffered much; ex-wife to John Dixon; formerly engaged to Dan Stewart, her "true love."

Dr. Jim Strasfield *(Geoffrey Horne):* a doctor with John Dixon's old job. He's attracted to Kim Dixon, but is willing to let her set the pace for their relationship.

Grant Colman *(James Douglas):* a lawyer; husband to Lisa; ex-husband to Joyce; natural father to Teddy Ellison. A very good man, but an oddball in that he's quiet, reserved, and supposedly very intelligent.

Lisa Shea Colman *(Eileen Fulton):* wife to Grant; ex-wife to Bob Hughes (and many others); mother to Tom and Chuck (off at school). She has turned from bitch to goddess over the years, but there's still the element of the busy-body; a stubborn and self-righteous woman; an interesting combination of good and evil.

Alma Miller *(Ethel Remey):* mother to Lisa; grandmother to Tom and Chuck. She knows her daughter's faults and is always ready to remind her of them.

Jay Stallings *(Dennis Cooney):* a business tycoon; estranged husband to Carol; in the past, the sometime lover of Susan Stewart and Natalie Bannon Hughes; a conniver who knows what is right, but can't help doing the wrong thing (if he can get away with it). He is a villain with one redeeming quality—his love for Carol.

Carol Stallings *(Rita McLaughlin):* estranged wife to Jay Stallings; ex-wife to Tom Hughes; a very sweet and naive young woman who's always willing to help others. She is a person with strong moral values.

Laurie Keaton *(Laurel Delmar):* secretary to Jay Stallings; a sensitive soul who's been hardened somewhat by watching her boss scheme and lie; a good person by any standard.

Mary Ellison *(Kelly Wood):* widow of Brian; adoptive mother to Teddy Ellison. She's a good mother, hardworking, honest, and good-natured; a proud sort who thinks the best of people.

Teddy Ellison *(Joseph Christopher):* adopted son to Mary Ellison; natural son to Grant and Joyce Colman (who were estranged at the time of his birth); about six years old.

Joyce Colman *(Barbara Rodell):* ex-wife to Grant; currently involved with Donald Hughes; a neurotic, insecure woman who causes problems for all who come her way.

Sandy Garrison *(Barbara Rucker):* ex-wife to Bob Hughes; widow of Norman Garrison; a kind and gentle woman who is dominated by her emotions. Played as a villain years ago, she has mellowed with age and no longer feels that her needs are more important than others'.

Kevin Thompson *(Michael Nader):* the mystery man in town; a playboy until he realized that he'd been wasting his life. He is a serious person who is in love with Susan Stewart, but cannot accept her deceits.

Dick Martin *(Ed Kemmer):* a lawyer to all; the third party in any situation. He is a man who knows what he wants and would like to have it—but he remains honorable.

Nurse Marion Connelly *(Clarice Blackburn):* a crusty older nurse with a soft spot for Bob Hughes; rough and tough, yet understanding and kind. She has a very strong sense of right and wrong.

Nurse Pat Holland *(Melinda Peterson):* a young nurse who has fallen for John Dixon; a confused sort, with good intentions.

DAYS OF OUR LIVES

Dr. Tom Horton, Sr. *(Macdonald Carey):* the good patriarch; husband to Alice; father to Bill, Mickey, Tom, Jr., and Marie (off in a convent); grandfather to Michael Jr., Julie, Jennifer Rose, Hope, and several others not presently seen; great-grandfather to David. He is the Most Respected Man in town, and a decent God-fearing sort.

Alice Horton *(Frances Reid):* the good matriarch; wife to Tom Sr; mother to Bill, Mickey, Tom Jr., and Marie; grandmother to Michael Jr., Julie, Jennifer Rose, and Hope, etc.; a religious woman, kind and compassionate. She and Tom have an ideal, old-fashioned marriage.

Mickey Horton *(John Clarke):* ex-husband to Laura and psychological father to Michael Jr.; reluctant husband to Maggie; son to Alice and Tom; brother to Bill, etc.; a good man full of trouble, for himself and others. He has suffered much from amnesia, psychological breakdowns, and bitterness.

Maggie "Hansen" Horton *(Suzanne Rogers):* wife to Mickey; a beautiful and hardworking farm girl, bewildered by the big city, and rejected by her husband (who married her during a spell of amnesia). Her enemy is Linda Patterson Phillips, who's after Mickey.

Dr. Bill Horton *(Ed Mallory):* husband to Laura; natural father to Michael Jr. and Jennifer Rose;

son to Alice and Tom; brother to Bill, etc.; a good man who, unlike his brother, has overcome life's difficulties. He and Laura have a "true love."

Dr. Laura Horton *(Rosemary Forsyth):* a psychiatrist; wife to Bill; mother to Michael Jr. and Jennifer Rose; ex-wife to Mickey; an independent and sensible woman. Due to guilt feelings, she is perhaps too involved in Mickey's rehabilitation.

Michael Horton, Jr. *(Wesley Eure):* illegitimate son to Bill and Laura (he had always thought that Mickey was his father). He is an impassioned young man who has suffered because of his parents' mistakes—and is now making them suffer.

Jennifer Rose Horton *(recasting):* small daughter to Laura and Bill; sister to Michael Horton, Jr.

Dr. Tom Horton, Jr. *(John Lupton):* a doctor who has seen his share of hard times; basically a good man.

Julie Anderson Williams *(Susan Seaforth Hayes):* wife to Doug Williams; mother to David Banning; daughter to Addie (deceased daughter of Alice and Tom) and therefore granddaughter to Alice and Tom; half-sister to Hope (by Addie and Doug Williams). She is the bitch who can turn goddess, but is usually somewhere in between; the always fascinating woman, and heroine of the story.

Doug Williams *(Bill Hayes):* owner of (and singer at) "Doug's Place," a nightclub/restaurant; husband to Julie (and formerly married to to her mother, Addie); father to Hope; a man with a playboy past, now a debonair family man. He and Julie have a "true love."

David Banning *(Richard Guthrie):* illegitimate son to Julie and Dave Martin; a bitter young man who is learning trust, love, and understanding the hard way. He is a source of worry to the Horton family; one reason is that he is romantically involved with a black girl, Valerie.

Hope Williams *(Natasha Ryan):* daughter to Doug Williams and the now-deceased Addie; the source of many of her father's worries even though she's only five or six years old.

Kim Williams *(Helen Funai):* ex-wife to Doug Williams. She recently turned up to cause him trouble; a "Polynesian Princess" who plays the game.

Robert LeClare *(Robert Clary):* Doug's French side-kick; husband to Rebecca; adoptive father to her newborn son Doug; a good and gentle soul with not a mean bone in his body.

Rebecca North LeClare *(Brooke Bundy):* housekeeper to Doug; wife to Robert LeClare; mother to little Doug (who is really Doug Williams' son, unbeknownst to him—it was done by artificial insemination, performed by Neil Curtis). She's an impulsive young woman who stumbles through life causing trouble.

Johnny Collins *(Paul Henry Itkins):* lover to Rebecca; a passionate young man who usually acts before he thinks.

Bob Anderson *(Mark Tapscott):* a good and sensitive businessman; ex-husband to Julie and Phyllis; father to Mary; natural father to Brooke Hamilton (by Adele Hamilton, who recently confessed all on the deathbed). He is always ready to protect those he loves.

Mary Anderson *(Barbara Stanger):* daughter to Bob and Phyllis; an insecure and sometimes aggressive young woman who must hide her fragile and kind-hearted nature to avoid being hurt. She is drawn to, but also repulsed by, her mother's husband.

Phyllis Anderson Curtis *(Corinne Conley):* wife to the much younger Neil Curtis; mother to Mary. She has suffered much—first from her husband's inattention, then from the death of a newborn son.

Dr. Neil Curtis *(Joe Gallison):* husband to Phyllis; partner to Greg Peters, and in love with his wife Amanda. The bad boy charmer; a compulsive gambler who is usually irresponsible. Fatherhood might have changed him.

Amanda Howard Peters *(Mary Frann):* wife to Greg Peters; best friend to Julie; a lovely but rather mixed-up woman who has learned slowly and painfully to deal with life. She had a long and troubled relationship with Neil Curtis.

Dr. Greg Peters *(Peter Brown):* the good doctor; husband to Amanda; ex-husband to Susan; decent and responsible.

Susan Peters *(Bennye Gatteys):* ex-wife to Greg; mother to little Ann; a woman filled with anxieties and every kind of neurosis imaginable. She is currently frigid and living with Eric Peters, Ann's father.

Eric Peters *(Stanley Kamel):* father to Ann; brother to Greg. He is an aggressive young man, driven by the desire to be his own man, and get out from under his brother's shadow.

Paul Grant *(Lawrence Cook):* patriarch of the only black family in town; husband to Helen; father to Danny and Valerie; surrogate father to David Banning; a decent and sensitive man. He is a reformed alcoholic employed as an accountant by Bob Anderson.

Helen Grant *(Ketty Lester):* wife to Paul; mother to Valerie and Danny; a God-fearing woman, strong and articulate where her family is concerned. She has pulled them through the hard times.

Danny Grant *(Hassan Shaheed, formerly known as Michael Dwight-Smith):* son to Helen and Paul; brother to Valerie; an intelligent black man, poor but proud. His ambition is to be a lawyer.

Valerie Grant *(Tina Andrews):* daughter to Helen and Paul; sister to Danny; an ambitious young black woman who is studying medicine. She is romantically involved with David Banning— which has everyone upset.

Don Craig *(Jed Allan):* the best lawyer in town; formerly fiancé to Julie, now interested in Marlene Evans. He is stubborn and tough—to some, a good friend and advisor.

Linda Patterson Phillips *(Margaret Mason):* a glamorous secretary who works in Don Craig's law offices; the villainous lady in town. Her one redeeming virtue is her love for Mickey.

Jeri Clayton *(Kaye Stevens):* estranged wife to Jack; mother to Trish; a weak-willed woman who's had a hard life and sometimes succumbs to self-pity. She has a good heart, and genuinely cares for her daughter.

Jack Clayton *(Jack Denbo):* an alcoholic; estranged husband to Jeri and stepfather to Trish. He beats his wife, covets his stepdaughter—and it's just a matter of time for him, poor soul.

Trish Clayton *(Patty Weaver):* an entertainer at "Doug's Place"; daughter to Jeri; stepdaughter to Jack; a girl of about twenty who is mixed-up, lonely, and afraid. Her relationships with men have been traumatic—love without sex, or vice versa.

Brooke Hamilton *(Adrienne LaRussa):* daughter to Adele (recently deceased) and Bob Anderson (a fact known only to her and Bob); the bad, bad girl—and it all stems from the fact that she's felt deprived and ashamed of her family all her life. She is trying to reform her ways, but it's not easy; ex-girlfriend to David Banning (and still in love with him); friend to Trish.

Dr. Marlene Evans *(Deirdre Hall):* the new psychiatrist in town; a smart and attractive woman, currently interested in Don Craig.

Karl Duval *(Alejandro Rey):* husband to Sharon; a rich, worldly and sophisticated man, with a French accent, and uncertain connections.

Sharon Duval *(Sally Stark):* wife to Karl; a patient of Dr. Evans; a game-player with an insatiable need for masculine attention.

Hank *(Ben DiTosti):* surrogate father to Maggie "Hansen" Horton; a real old-time farm boy. He's romancing Rosie.

Rosie *(Fran Ryan):* Laura and Bill's housekeeper and Jennifer Rose's nanny. She's being romanced by two old codgers, Hank and Nathan.

Nathan Curtis *(Tom Brown):* father to Neil Curtis; a compulsive gambler who is making a play for Rosie—but only for her money. He's an untrustworthy sort, but his new-found affection for his son seems to be changing him for the better.

THE DOCTORS

Dr. Matt Powers *(James Pritchett):* husband to Maggie; father to Mike and Greta; grandfather to Michael Paul. He's the good doctor and patriarch of the show; generally a kind and idealistic man, but the burden of responsibility at the hospital has made him seem sterner and more practical (ruthless) than he really is.

Dr. Maggie Powers *(Lydia Bruce):* a good doctor; wife to Matt; stepmother to Mike; mother to Greta.

She stands by her husband through thick and thin.

Dr. Mike Powers (*Armand Assante*): a doctor now working as a policeman; husband to Toni; son to Matt; stepson to Maggie; a former drug addict and problem child. He's reformed somewhat.

Toni Powers (*recasting*): a young medical researcher; wife to Mike; best friend to Martha Allen; a mixed-up girl, but good-hearted.

Greta Powers (*Jennifer Houlton*): a teenager; daughter to Maggie and Matt; half-sister to Mike; currently dating Billie. She has all the teenage problems one could imagine.

Dr. Althea Davis (*Elizabeth Hubbard*): mother to Penny; best friend to Maggie and Matt; a good doctor and our heroine—even though she's stubborn, aggressive, etc.

Penny Davis (*Julia Duffy*): daughter to Althea; the problem child grown up. She seems to be changing into a more level-headed young woman.

Mona Aldrich Croft (*Meg Mundy*): the richest lady in town; mother to Steve Aldrich; grandmother to Erich and Stephanie; also called "grandmother" by Billy and Stacy. She's a schemer and an upper-class snob; not really an "evil" person in that what she does is done for her family—if only her judgments on what is right were not so often wrong!

Dr. Steve Aldrich (*David O'Brien*): our hero; estranged husband to Carolee; father to Erich; stepfather to Billie; son to Mona; the current love object of Ann Larimer and MJ Match. He is a decent man who tries to do what's best but doesn't always succeed.

Nurse Carolee Aldrich (*Jada Rowland*): estranged wife to Steve Aldrich; mother to Stephanie; stepmother to Billy and Erich; cousin to MJ Match; a volatile person—decent, loving and admired by all. She has recently suffered a breakdown as a result of marital problems.

Stephanie Aldrich (*Bridget Breen*): daughter to Steve and Carolee, about five years old, and rarely seen.

Erich Aldrich (*Keith Blanchard*): son to Steve; grandson to Mona; a very mixed-up boy. He has had problems adjusting to the behavior of the adults around him.

Billy Allison (*David Elliott*): a teenager; foster son to Steve; romantically involved with Greta Powers. He's been at loose ends ever since his stepparents broke up; but a very nice boy nonetheless.

Jason Aldrich (*Glenn Corbett*): son to Mona; brother to Steve; stepfather to Stacy; a high-powered lawyer and golden boy of the family.

Stacy Wells Summers (*Leslie Ann Ray*): wife to Paul Summers; niece to Steve Aldrich; "granddaughter" to Mona; a very spacy mixed-up girl; a schemer who's involved with drugs. Her sexual hang-ups and insecurities are too numerous to mention.

Dr. Paul Summers (*Paul Carr*): a villainous doctor; husband to Stacy. He is using Stacy and Ann Larimer to gain his own evil ends, and is being used in return; an immoral and emotionally unstable man.

Eleanor Conrad (*Lois Smith*): widow of Scott Conrad; mother to Wendy (who's away at school); a good woman but a bit naive about the world. She was recently released from a mental institution, and has made a remarkable adjustment to the real world; currently being charmed by Lew Dancy.

Virginia Dancy (*Elizabeth Lawrence*): housekeeper to Mona Croft and the Aldrich family; mother to Lew, Sarah, Nola, and Jerry; a hardworking woman on her own.

Lew Dancy (*Frank Telfer*): son to Virginia; brother to Sarah, Nola, and Jerry. He is a lazy, scheming sort, always looking for something for nothing.

Sarah Dancy (*Antoinette Panneck*): daughter to Virginia; sister to Lew, Nola, and Jerry. She is a sweet young thing who looks only for the best in people; a friend to Penny Davis.

Nola Dancy (*Kathryn Harrold*): daughter to Virginia; sister to Lew, Sarah, and Jerry. She grew up the hard way and has bitter feelings about her life; a tough young woman who is loyal to her friends and family.

Jerry Dancy (*Jonathan Hogan*): son to Virginia; brother to Lew, Sarah, and Nola; an earnest young law student. A recent development—he married Penny Davis!

Dr. Ann Larimer (*Geraldine Court*): a decent

doctor turned bad by her lust for Steve Aldrich; a blackmailer, schemer, conniver.

Martha Allen *(Sally Gracie):* a middle-aged medical researcher; overly talkative, but well-meaning; a trustworthy sort; best friend to Toni Powers.

Ernie Cadman *(George Smith):* a police officer; romantically involved with Martha; rarely seen.

Dr. Hank Iverson *(Palmer Deane):* a respected doctor; the only black in town; an idealist.

Nurse Mary Jane ("MJ") Match *(Lauren White):* cousin to Carolee; a good and kindly young woman; romantically involved with Steve Aldrich; the vulnerable type.

THE EDGE OF NIGHT

Mike Karr *(Forrest Compton):* a lawyer; husband to Nancy; father to Laurie; grandfather to newborn John Victor; a very good man, well-respected by all.

Nancy Karr *(Ann Flood):* wife to Mike; step-mother to Laurie; a good woman with a small rebellious streak. Due to the mob, she has experienced unexpected troubles in her marriage.

Laurie Karr Dallas *(Linda Cook):* wife to Johnny; mother to newborn John Victor; daughter to Mike; stepdaughter to Ann; a nice girl whose only fault is that she can be very selfish.

Johnny Dallas *(John LaGioia):* husband to Laurie; father to newborn John Victor; brother to Tracy Dallas Micelli; a tough guy from the wrong side of the tracks who went straight after a jail sentence. He helps good triumph over evil.

Tracy Micelli *(Pat Conwell):* estranged wife to Danny; a former prostitute and a gold-digger. She went straight after a few mistakes—and after falling in love with Danny and the good life.

Danny Micelli *(Lou Criscuolo):* estranged husband to Tracy; a good guy, comically tough, and very endearing in his shy way.

Bill Marceau *(Mandel Kramer):* the Chief of Police. He helps Mike Karr on special assignments.

Lt. Luke Chandler *(Herb Davis):* a black police officer; a good man who takes his work seriously.

Kevin Jamison *(John Driver):* a newspaper reporter; widower of Phoebe, recently deceased; heir to the Whitney fortune. He is a nice young man, but too emotionally dependent on Geraldine Whitney.

Geraldine Whitney *(Lois Kibbee):* at sixty or so, the richest lady in town. She is nice, stubborn, spoiled, and sometimes stern; a widow who lost two sons, and has taken Kevin under her wing.

John *(George Hall):* husband to Trudy; the perfect butler. He's been with the Whitney family for years.

Trudy *(Mary Hayden):* wife to John; the perfect maid and sometimes confidante of Mrs. Whitney. She and John see and hear all but never, ever tell.

Adam Drake *(Donald May):* husband to Nicole; friend to the Karrs; law partner to Mike Karr. He is a kind and understanding man, with a very strong moral code (his problems are caused by Fate).

Nicole Travis Drake *(Maeve McGuire):* wife to Adam; employee of Johnny; a very nice woman. She and Adam have a "true love."

Olivia Brandeis ("Brandy") Henderson *(Dixie Carter):* a very good lawyer and an assistant D.A.. She was at one time happily engaged to Adam; however the break-up of that romance (Nicole returned from the dead) transformed her into a vengeful woman. She can't last long that way.

Dr. Chris Neely *(Douglas Warner):* a young psychologist; a newcomer who seems charming and comical.

Dr. Clay Jordon *(Niles McMaster):* a bogus doctor; a murderer; a wolf in sheep's clothing.

Draper Scott *(Tony Craig):* an assistant D.A.; son to Ansel Scott; romantically interested in Brandy. He's a handsome, charming young man whose emotional problems stem from an overbearing and manipulative father; a gullible sort—and that could lead him into trouble.

Ansel Scott *(Patrick Horgan):* the overbearing father to Draper; fiancé to Nadine Alexander; a cold and calculating man.

Nadine Alexander *(Dorothy Stinnette):* fiancée to Ansel; mother to Raven. An upper-crust woman whose motives and character are uncertain; probably a schemer.

Raven Alexander *(Juanin Clay):* daughter to Nadine; a very cosmopolitan young woman who is chasing Draper (though involved with Ansel); a nice girl with ulterior motives.

Steve Guthrie *(Denny Albee):* a police officer who

was hired by Adam to protect Nicole; a good man, if a bit headstrong.

Tony Saxon *(Louis Turrene):* the head of the Underworld in Monticello; a cruel and powerful man. His only weakness is his daughter, Deborah, who wraps Daddy around her little finger.

Deborah Saxon *(Frances Fisher):* daughter to Tony Saxon; a spoiled young woman with a cruel streak. She's accustomed to getting her way (but may have met her match in Danny Micelli).

Molly O'Conner *(Helena Carroll):* a tough policewoman with the proverbial heart of gold. She was secretly hired by Adam to keep an eye on Nicole.

GENERAL HOSPITAL

Dr. Steve Hardy *(John Beradino):* the Chief of Staff at General Hospital; currently (and perhaps illegally) husband to Audrey, and, much to his surprise, natural father to Jeff Webber. He is aware of his responsibilities as a doctor and a human being—and tries hard to satisfy both whenever possible.

Nurse Jessie Brewer *(Emily McLaughlin):* ex-wife to many; a sweet and sympathetic person who always wears a white sweater. She has suffered much over the years, mostly because she always seems to get involved with the wrong man.

Dr. Peter Taylor *(Craig Huebing):* the good and decent psychiatrist; husband to Diana Taylor; stepfather to Martha; best friend to Lesley Faulkner. He has made his share of mistakes, but somehow they are never his fault; an intelligent and generally sensible man.

Nurse Diana Taylor *(Valerie Starrett):* wife to Peter Taylor; mother to Martha (as a result of her having been raped by Phil Brewer, Jessie's long-dead husband); a good woman, but insecure and uncertain about her ability to cope.

Martha Taylor *(Lisa Lyke):* school-aged daughter to Diana; hardly ever seen.

Mike *(Dennis Simster):* the school-aged child Peter and Diana might adopt. He is hostile and defensive, but Peter feels that with, love and care, he will adjust happily.

Dr. Lesley Faulkner *(Denise Alexander):* the heroine; widow of Cameron Faulkner, recently deceased, and pregnant with his child; an innocent, idealistic woman with a heart of gold; long-lost natural mother to Laura.

Dr. Adam Streeter *(Brett Halsey):* Lesley's obstetrician; a newcomer.

Terri Arnett *(Bobbi Jordan):* a singer; big sister to Rick and Jeff Webber; sister-in-law to Monica; currently in love with Mark Dante. She provides the necessary shoulder to all who enter her little nightclub; a good woman.

Dr. Rick Webber *(Michael Gregory):* the brilliant young doctor; brother to Terri and Jeff; protégé of Steve Hardy; lover to Monica. He is an idealistic young man who gets entangled in other people's intrigues.

Dr. Jeff Webber *(Richard Dean Anderson):* estranged husband to Monica; younger brother to Rick and Terri; an insecure young man presently popping pills to solve his problems; it now seems he's Steve Hardy's natural son. Will that help?

Dr. Monica Webber *(Patsy Rahn):* estranged wife to Jeff; sister-in-law to Terri and to Rick (her lover). She is very insecure—and that gets her into trouble; in all, a very childish young woman.

Audrey Hobart *(Rachel Ames):* wife to many, most recently to Steve Hardy (perhaps illegally, since the status of an ex-husband is unclear); mother to Tommy; a good woman who has suffered many hardships. She lacks confidence in herself and in life.

Tommy Hobart (*David Comfort*): son to Audrey and Tom Baldwin; about nine years old. He has been hurt and confused by his parents' marital troubles, and blames his mother for driving away his stepfather.

Dr. Tom Baldwin (*Don Chastain*): father to Tommy; ex-husband to Audrey; a once-evil man who caused much grief for Audrey. Accused of killing a man, he spent many months in a Mexican jail before getting his freedom and returning to Port Charles; now, perhaps, reformed.

Heather Grant (*Georganne La Piere*): a scheming young girl who's determined to get herself a rich husband, no matter whom she destroys in the process.

Dr. Mark Dante (*Gerald Gordon*): an independent, strong-willed and extremely likeable surgeon; romantically interested in Terri Arnett, but determined to stay with his mentally-ill wife, Mary Ellen, because he feels responsible for her illness.

Mary Ellen Dante (*Lee Warrick*): wife to Mark; a mentally disturbed woman.

Dr. Gina Dante (*Anna Stuart*): sister to Mark Dante; a gynecologist who works with Adam Streeter; a good doctor and a nice person.

Jill Streeter (*not cast*): sixteen-year-old daughter to Adam Streeter, a young girl who has become very possessive of her father since her mother's death.

Laura Vining (*not cast*): long-lost daughter to Leslie Faulkner; a nice girl but a bit confused by recent revelations about her parentage.

Dr. Gail Adamson (*not cast*): a good doctor; former mentor to Monica Webber.

Lee Baldwin (*Peter Hansen*): husband to Carolyn Chandler; stepfather to Bobby Chandler; a kind-hearted lawyer devoted to family and friends.

GUIDING LIGHT

Bert Bauer (*Charita Bauer*): a good-natured matriarch; a widow; mother to Mike and Ed; grandmother to Freddie, Christina and Hope; an old-fashioned sort who always worries about her children.

Mike Bauer (*Don Stewart*): a lawyer; widower of Leslie; father to Hope; stepfather to Freddie; a good and kind man.

Hope Bauer (*Robin Mattson*): daughter to Mike; granddaughter to Bert; a willful young girl who resents her father's protective interference. She is romantically involved with Ben McFarren.

Dr. Ed Bauer (*Mart Hulswit*): ex-husband to Holly; father to Freddie; son to Bert; a good doctor who went bad (alcoholism) when Fate stepped in to ruin his life. He's back on the straight and narrow, and very interested in Rita Stapleton.

Freddie Bauer (*Gary Hannoch*): son to Ed and Leslie (previous marriage); about seven years old; a good little boy.

Holly Norris Bauer (*Maureen Garrett*): ex-wife to Ed; mother to Christina; daughter to Barbara Thorpe; a good girl gone bad and back again. She is weak, but through suffering has learned to be better, stronger.

Christina Bauer (*Gina Foy*): daughter to Holly and, to all appearances, Ed; but Roger Thorpe is her natural father.

Barbara Thorpe (*Barbara Berjer*): a nice middle-aged lady who is too involved in daughter Holly's problems. She resents Roger (her husband's son and daughter's ex-lover).

Adam Thorpe (*Robert Milli*): husband to Barbara; father to Roger; stepfather to Holly; a handsome, intelligent middle-aged man. He has had to suffer his wife's neuroses.

Roger Thorpe (*Michael Zaslow*): husband to Peggy Fletcher; stepfather to Billy; ex-lover to Holly. He is Peck's bad boy, but charming.

Nurse Peggy Fletcher Thorpe (*Fran Myers*): a nice nurse; wife to Roger; mother to Billy. She knows all, forgives all.

Billy Fletcher (*Shane Nickerson*): son to Peggy; a young boy who idolizes his stepfather, Roger.

Dr. Sarah McIntyre (Werner) (*Millette Alexander*): a nice doctor; widow of Joe Werner, recently deceased; foster mother to "T.J."

T. J. Werner (*T. J. Hargrave*): a young boy with a mysterious past which has apparently hardened him somewhat. He found love and happiness with the Werners.

Nurse Rita Stapleton (*Lenore Kasdorf*): a kind and helpful nurse; daughter to Viola; sister to Eve; currently in love with Ed Bauer. She is a girl from a poor family who is determined to live a better life than her parents.

Eve Stapleton (*Janet Grey*): daughter to Viola; sister to Rita; a sweet young country girl.

Viola Stapleton (*Kate Wilkinson*): mother to Rita and Eve; a good down-to-earth woman.

Ann Jeffers (*Maureen Mooney*): a lonely, insecure woman who found a friend in Mike Bauer. She is looking for her long-lost son, Jimmy.

Dr. Stephen Jackson (*Stefan Schnabel*): hot-shot older doctor, and the show's patriarch. He speaks his mind no matter what the consequences.

Ben McFarren (*Stephen Yates*): brother to Jerry; an ex-convict who was wrongly imprisoned; a very determined and hot-headed young man; currently dating Hope Bauer.

Jerry McFarren (*Peter Jensen*): brother to Ben; a young man who's confused, mixed-up, and in trouble.

Raymond Shafer (*Keith Aldrich*): a lawyer investigating the death of Malcolm Granger.

Dr. Justin Marler (*Tom O'Rourke*): an excellent surgeon; a former beau to Sarah McIntyre Werner; an arrogant, aggressive man.

Jacqueline Marler (*not cast*): wealthy ex-wife to Justin.

LOVE OF LIFE

Mayor Bruce Sterling (*Ron Tomme*): decent, upright mayor of Rosehill; husband to Vanessa; grandfather to Hank. He has had several flings in the past, but his marriage has always survived; a good man who only occasionally succumbs to temptation.

Vanessa Sterling (*Audrey Peters*): the long-suffering good sister of Meg Hart; wife to Bruce Sterling; daughter to Sarah Caldwell; aunt to Ben and Cal. She is half of a model marriage; a kind and sympathetic person.

Meg Dale Hart (*Tudi Wiggins*): the evil and wealthy sister to Vanessa; ex-wife to Edouard Aleata; mother to Cal and Ben; grandmother to Ben's illegitimate child Suzanne. She believes that money can buy anything and loves to manipulate people "for their own good"; in love with Rick Latimer, her son-in-law.

Sarah Caldwell (*Joanna Roos*): mother to Vanessa and Meg; grandmother to Cal and Ben; a matriarch.

Caroline ("Cal") Aleata Latimer (*Roxanne Gregory*): wife to Rick Latimer; daughter to Meg Hart; sister to Ben; a sweet innocent who has learned to be tougher, but not tough enough.

Rick Latimer (*Jerry Lacy*): husband to Cal; father to Hank; a thoroughly charming blackguard; owner of "Beaver Ridge." He can be very evil, but only when he has a major stake in something; otherwise he's not too objectionable.

Hank Latimer (*David Carlton Stambaugh*): a boy of about thirteen; son to Rick; grandson to Bruce Sterling. He is very understanding of his father's faults, and so the two have a good relationship.

Ben Harper (*Chandler Hill Harben*): a product of one of Meg's marriages; father to Betsy's illegitimate child Suzanne; half-brother to Cal; ex-husband to Arlene. He is a charming scoundrel, recently released from prison (for bigamy) and eager to change his ways for love of Betsy.

Betsy Crawford (*Elizabeth Kemp*): sister to Tom Crawford; temporarily "wife" to Ben (it wasn't legal, since he hadn't divorced Arlene); mother to Ben's newborn child Suzanne. She is a sweet innocent, who was crushed by Ben's lies and deceptions; now somewhat bitter and tougher.

Dr. Tom Crawford (*Richard K. Weber*): brother to Betsy, and her defender; athletic, charming, intelligent. He is Carrie's doctor.

Arlene Lovett (*Birgitta Tolksdorf*): ex-wife to Ben Harper; daughter to Carrie. She is a poor girl gone bad; but there's a heart of gold underneath all the armor.

Carrie Lovett (*Peg Murray*): long-suffering mother to Arlene; perhaps Meg Hart's only friend. She is a good, strong, and independent woman who worries about her daughter and tries to get her on the "right track."

Ray Slater (*Lloyd Battista*): a black-shirt, white-tie sort of villain; a gambler with few redeeming qualities. When trouble starts, he doesn't expect anyone to help "people like us."

Edouard Aleata (*John Aniston*): ex-husband to Meg; stepfather to Cal; a charming, continental type, decent and caring. He has fallen for a married woman, Felicia Lamont.

Charles Lamont (*Jonathan Moore*): husband to Felicia; grandfather to Johnny; ex-husband to Diana; a frustrated, selfish, at times overbearing man. He lost Diana because of his sexual problems, then married Felicia, only to find that she was too hung up to consummate the marriage!

Felicia Flemming Lamont (*Pamela Lincoln*): wife to Charles (in name only); a very confused woman who, mistaking her husband for a would-be rapist, shot him. She's fallen for Edouard, but has sworn to take care of Charles for life.

Johnny Prentiss (*Trip Randall*): a sensible boy about twelve years old; grandson to Charles.

Dr. Joe Cusak (*Peter Brouwer*): doctor to Charles Lamont and Lynn Henderson; a charming, idealistic man, dedicated to his work.

Lynn Henderson (*Amy Gibson*): a teenage alcoholic whom Vanessa has taken under her wing.

Ian Russell (*Michael Allinson*): a continental charmer with certain criminal connections; co-owner of "Beaver Ridge"; attracted to Arlene Lovett.

Vivian Carlson (*Helene Dumas*): a wealthy, conniving, meddlesome older woman; she has not been seen for years.

ONE LIFE TO LIVE

Joe Riley (*Lee Patterson*): the good guy; ace newspaperman; husband to Vicky; father to newborn Kevin. He had an affair with Cathy Craig, which produced a child, Megan, who was killed in an auto accident with Vicky.

Victoria ("Vicky") Lord Riley (*Erika Slezak*): wife to Joe; mother to newborn Kevin; half-sister to Tony Lord; a wealthy young woman. She is our heroine, beloved by all—except her mortal enemy, Cathy Craig Lord.

Cathy Craig Lord (*Jennifer Harmon*): once an ace writer, now incapacitated by neurotic problems; wife to Tony Lord; daughter to Jim Craig; stepdaughter to Anna. She is an impetuous, somewhat bitter young woman who has caused trouble in the past and will do so again; a feminist.

Tony Lord (*George Reinholt*): husband to Cathy; half-brother to Vicky; lover to Pat Kendall (then and now) and unbeknownst to him, the father of her son Brian. He is a charming rascal with a heart of gold.

Dr. Jim Craig (*Nat Polen*): husband to Anna Wolek; long-suffering father to Cathy; brother-in-law to Vinnie and Larry. He is the patriarch, loving and understanding.

Anna Wolek Craig (*Doris Belack*): wife to Jim Craig; stepmother to Cathy; older sister to Larry and Vinnie, and a surrogate mother to them. She is a very good woman; a matriarch.

Vince ("Vinnie") Wolek (*Jordan Charney*): a well-intentioned policeman; husband to Wanda; brother to Larry and Anna; a male chauvinist with a stormy temper.

Wanda Webb Wolek (*Marilyn Chris*): wife to Vinnie, and the calming force in his life; an employee of Tony Lord. She and Vince are similar to Archie and Edith Bunker on *All in the Family*, only much nicer and more realistic; they provide lots of humor.

Nurse Jenny Wolek Siegel *(Katherine Glass)*: a nun who left the convent to marry her true love, Tim Siegel (subsequently killed during an argument with Vinnie); a cousin to the Wolek family; a sweet, strong and intelligent young woman.

Dr. Larry Wolek *(Michael Storm)*: fiancé to Karen, his cousin; father to Danny; brother to Anna and Vinnie; ex-brother-in-law to Vicky, and her secret admirer; a level-headed, caring person.

Karen Wolek *(Kathryn Breech)*: fiancée to Larry, her cousin; sister to Jenny Wolek Siegel. She is a young woman out for herself; a scheming selfish type.

Danny Wolek *(Neail Holland)*: son to Larry Wolek and his now-deceased wife, Meredith Lord; a school-aged boy who isn't much involved in the story, except as a possible stumbling block or future problem for Larry and Karen.

Dr. Dorian Cramer Lord *(Nancy Pinkerton)*: stepmother to Tony and Vicky, and about their age. She is the true "bitch" (it's surprising she's lasted this long); scheming, vindictive, underhanded, rotten.

Dr. Peter Janssen *(Jeffrey Pomerantz)*: a good doctor who might turn bad if it gets him what he wants—Jenny Siegel; a man full of self-importance, and yearning for money and power.

Lt. Ed Hall *(Al Freeman, Jr.)*: a good and honest policeman; husband to Carla and head of the only black family in town.

Carla Hall *(Ellen Holly)*: secretary to Jim Craig; wife to Lt. Hall; a good black woman, strong-willed and stubborn.

Patricia Kendall *(Jacqueline Courtney)*: a reporter; mother to Brian; a good and decent woman who once had an affair with Tony Lord and has recently resumed it; a friend to Vicky.

Brian Kendall *(Stephen Austin)*: son to Patricia—and to Tony (unbeknownst to him and Tony); about eleven years old. He is very introspective and sensitive, and this could lead to trouble.

Dr. Will Vernon *(Farley Granger)*: a new psychiatrist in town; husband to Naomi; father to Brad and Samantha; a good man with family problems. He has an eye for women—especially for his nurse Jenny Siegel.

Naomi Vernon *(Teri Keane)*: wife to Will; mother to Brad and Samantha. She has trouble coping with her husband's career, and his real or imagined infidelities.

Brad Vernon *(Jameson Parker)*: a professional tennis player on the make; son to Naomi and Will; brother to Samantha; an arrogant young man with women first and foremost on his mind.

Samantha Vernon *(Julie Montgomery)*: daughter to Naomi and Will; sister to Brad.

Matt McAllister *(Vance Jefferis)*: an unscrupulous man; a cohort of Dorian Cramer Lord. He is essentially a coward, but can maneuver his way to the top with a certain flair.

Lana McLain *(Jackie Zeman)*: a waitress at "Tony's Place." She's in love with Brad Vernon, who's leading her down the primrose path.

RYAN'S HOPE

Johnny Ryan *(Bernard Barrow)*: patriarch of the Ryan clan; husband to Maeve; father to Frank, Mary, Pat (and a few others not seen); grandfather to little John; a traditional Catholic with a big heart and the proverbial Irish wit and temper.

Maeve Ryan *(Helen Gallagher)*: matriarch of the Ryan clan; wife to Johnny; mother to Frank, Mary, Pat, etc.; grandmother to little John; as traditional as her husband, but a bit more tolerant.

She is a kind and stronghearted woman with a sense of humor and an unshakeable faith.

Frank Ryan *(Andrew Robinson)*: a politician reminiscent of the Kennedys (but now in decline); estranged husband to Delia; father to Little John; son to Maeve and Johnny; brother to Mary and Pat; lover to Jill Coleridge. He is a decent and impassioned man who will do the "right thing" if he can.

Delia Reid Ryan *(Ilene Kristen):* estranged wife to Frank; mother to little John; sister to Bob Reid; ex-lover to Roger Coleridge and Pat Ryan (her high school sweetheart); a spoiled and insecure child/woman with a dangerous habit of getting her way. She worships the Ryans for the family values she never had as a child.

Bob Reid *(Earl Hindman):* a big Irish policeman; brother to Delia; friend and former colleague to Frank; a calm man with sensible, traditional ideas.

Mary Ryan Fenelli *(Kate Mulgrew):* a TV reporter; wife to Jack (and pregnant with his child); daughter to Maeve and Johnny; sister to Frank and Pat. She is a good girl torn between Jack's irreverent ways and her parents' traditional values.

Jack Fenelli *(Michael Levin):* a reporter; husband to Mary and unwilling father to her unborn child; currently an invalid recovering from auto injuries that may leave him with "sexual dysfunction." Life as an orphan left him defensive and jealous of love; he is determined to have Mary to himself—which never happens.

Dr. Pat Ryan *(Malcolm Groome):* an intern in neurology; son to Maeve and Johnny; brother to Frank and Mary; sometime love interest of Delia and Faith Coleridge. He's handsome and full of charm—but there's a wild streak that can cause problems.

Jillian ("Jill") Coleridge *(Nancy Addison):* an outstanding lawyer; sister to Faith and Roger; lover to Frank, and briefly involved with Seneca Beaulac (which resulted in pregnancy). She is a strong, imaginative woman who feels impelled to act on moral principles—at some cost to herself.

Dr. Roger Coleridge *(Ron Hale):* brother to Jill and Faith; a wealthy, idle bachelor, who lies, cheats—and is surprised when no one sympathizes with his behavior. His only excuse was his genuine love for faithless Delia.

Dr. Faith Coleridge *(Catherine Hicks):* an intern in pediatrics; sister to Jill and Roger; friend and lover to Pat. She was transformed from a sweet, naive girl into a paranoid; now cured, she seems stronger for the ordeal she has been through.

Dr. Clem Moultrie *(Hannibal Penney, Jr.):* a sort of foster brother to Jill, Roger and Faith; the protégé/son their father needed to make up for the rascally Roger. He is the only black man around—a brilliant surgeon and an idealist.

Dr. Seneca Beaulac *(John Gabriel):* wealthy widower of Bucky's Aunt Nell; a compelling man, with serious purposes—and a sense of fun. He was recently convicted for having pulled the respirator plug on his dead-but-breathing wife; now working as a doctor/administrator and courting Jill.

Dr. Bucky Carter *(Justin Deas):* an intern in neurology; best friend to Pat and heir to thirty million. He is sensitive about his money; a nice young man who has been taken advantage of in the past.

Dr. Alex McLean *(Ed Evanko):* a young widower; an old army buddy of Jack Fenelli, and currently his doctor. He gets along with Mary and the Ryans ever so much better than Jack does.

SEARCH FOR TOMORROW

Jo Vincente *(Mary Stuart):* the heroine for over twenty-five years, and veteran of many romances and marriages; adoptive mother to Bruce; mother to Patti Whiting; sister to the recently murdered Eunice Wyatt and a friend to all.

Bruce Carson *(Joel Higgins):* an ace reporter; husband to Amy; father to Victoria (out of wedlock); adoptive son to Jo Vincente; a good man. Although he blunders at times, it's always with the best of intentions.

Dr. Amy Kaslo Carson *(Anne Wyndham):* wife to Bruce; mother to Victoria ("Tory"); sister to Steve. She is a sweet innocent with a will of iron.

Steve Kaslo *(Michael Nouri):* husband to Liza; brother to Amy; a vagabond who changed his ways when he found love and happiness with Liza; now a strong and independent young man battling leukemia.

Liza Walton Kaslo *(Meg Bennett):* a fashion model;

wife to Steve; daughter to Janet Collins; step-daughter to Wade; and sister to Gary and Danny. She's a sweet ingenue who worries about everyone and everything.

Dr. Gary Walton *(Rick Lohman):* a young, idealistic doctor; son to Janet Collins; stepson to Wade; brother to Liza and Danny; a good sort with a strong sense of values; the kind of son any parent would be proud of.

Janet Collins *(Millee Taggart):* wife to Wade; mother to Gary, Liza and Danny; a very nice woman, but a little stubborn and righteous.

Wade Collins *(John Cunningham):* husband to Janet; father to Danny; stepfather to Gary and Liza; a family man in a nice family. Nonetheless, he is sometimes insecure and indecisive.

Danny Walton *(Neil Billingsley):* son to Janet and Wade; about six years old.

John Wyatt *(Val Dufour):* widower of Eunice, recently murdered; brother-in-law to Jo Vincente; stepfather to Susie. His past affair with Jennifer Pace resulted in her murdering his wife.

Jennifer Pace *(Morgan Fairchild):* a clutching, weak young woman who has only her looks to get her by; a schemer who's "in love" with the older John Wyatt. She thinks the world is against her and has responded by taking men from best friends and happy families; not very discriminating in her search for a father figure.

Walter Pace *(Tom Klunis):* husband to Stephanie Collins; father to Jennifer; an arrogant, aggressive and unprincipled man. He married Stephanie for her money.

Stephanie Collins Pace *(Marie Cheatham):* wife to Walter Pace; widow of Clay Collins; ex-wife to Dave Wilkins and mother to Wendy. She is a scheming, greedy woman who always wants her own way—but she tends to get involved with men stronger and more devious than she.

Wendy Wilkins *(Andrea McArdle):* daughter to Stephanie and Dave Wilkins; a good little girl who puts up with her mother's instabilities and

actually likes her; too young to be of any real trouble.

Patti Whiting *(Tina Sloan):* wife to Len; daughter to Jo Vincente; a selfish, mixed-up young woman who has created problems for those who love her.

Dr. Len Whiting *(Dino Narizzano):* husband to Patti; son-in-law to Jo Vincente; a weak but good man. His wife's insecurities and problems have led him to make mistakes in the past.

Scott Phillips *(Peter Simon):* husband to Kathy; ex-husband to Jennifer; foster father to Eric Leshinsky; a reformed alcoholic. He tends to be weaker than his wife, but comes through very well in a pinch.

Kathy Phillips *(Courtney Sherman):* a good lawyer; wife to Scott Phillips; a strong-willed woman who puts her career right up there with her marriage.

Eric Leshinsky *(Chris Lowe):* foster son to Scott Phillips; basically a nice young boy. Though he can be troublesome, Kathy and Scott can usually handle him.

Stu Bergman *(Larry Haines):* husband to Elly; father to Janet and Tommy; grandfather to Gary, Liza, and Danny; co-owner of "The Hartford House" (with best friend Jo Vincente). He is a good old sort, a friend to all.

Elly Harper Bergman *(Billie Lou Watt):* wife to Stu; distant cousin to Scott Phillips; a good woman, though a bit shy and self-effacing.

Dr. Bob Rogers *(Carl Low):* a head doctor at the hospital. A good man and a friend to all, especially Jo Vincente.

David Sutton *(Lewis Arlt):* an ace private detective; a strong and very tough young man.

Woody Reed *(Kevin Kline):* an owner of a modeling agency. He is trying to make Liza a top model.

Gail Caldwell *(Sherry Rooney):* co-worker of Bruce Carson.

Stuart Brooks *(Robert Colbert):* owner of the newspaper; the middle-aged patriarch in town; husband to Jennifer; father to Leslie, Chris, Peggy and psychological father to Laurie (she's really Bruce Henderson's daughter—a fact Stuart just learned); a real family man.

Jennifer Brooks *(Dorothy Green):* the middle-aged matriarch in town; wife to Stuart; mother to Leslie, Laurie, Chris, and Peggy. She is a good woman and, in many ways, strong and independent.

Lauralee ("Laurie") Brooks Prentiss *(Jaime Lyn Bauer):* a novelist; one of the Brooks sisters; wife to Lance; a bad girl who has reformed, but is still a little too worldly for her own good.

Lance Prentiss *(John McCook):* a very wealthy arrogant young businessman; husband to Laurie; son to Vanessa; brother to Lucas. He seems to be drawn to his sister-in-law, Leslie; not a "good man," but attractive nonetheless.

Lucas Prentiss *(not cast):* son to Vanessa; brother to Lance; the black sheep of the family.

Vanessa Prentiss *(K.T. Stevens):* mother to Lance and Lucas. She always wears veils to hide a deformity; seemingly bitter and ruthless.

Leslie Brooks Eliot *(Victoria Mallory):* a concert pianist; one of the Brooks sisters; estranged wife to Brad Eliot. She was transformed from a shy, innocent girl, to an independent, charming woman with a career of her own. She and Brad have a "true love."

Brad Eliot *(Tom Hallick):* estranged husband to Leslie; a psychiatrist turned reporter; a "good" man but torn by guilt and worry and more than one human weakness. He is currently losing his sight, and is determined not to become a burden.

Chris Brooks Foster *(Trish Stewart):* one of the Brooks sisters; wife to Snapper; a beautiful, bright and caring young woman. She and Snapper have a "true love."

Dr. Snapper Foster *(David Hasselhoff):* husband to Chris; son to Liz; brother to Greg and Jill. He is a quiet, determined man who cares deeply for his family and his work, but tries not to let it show.

Peggy Brooks *(Pam Peters Solow):* a college student; one of the Brooks sisters; fiancée to Jack Curtis; a sweet and earnest type.

Jack Curtis (Curtzynski) *(Anthony Herrera):* ex-husband to Joann; fiancé to Peggy; in the past, a selfish, inconsiderate man.

Joann Curtzynski *(Kay Heberle):* ex-wife to Jack; friend and employee of Brock Reynolds. She is fighting obesity and lack of self-esteem; an insecure young woman who is learning to cope with life all over again.

Brock Reynolds *(Beau Kayzer):* son to Kay Chancellor; formerly a rascal, now friend to all. He found God a few years ago and has been trying to reform people ever since with a philosophy of "Love Thyself and Thy Neighbor."

Kay Chancellor *(Jeanne Cooper):* mother to Brock Reynolds; the wealthiest woman in town; a reformed alcoholic; insecure, lonely and selfish.

Liz Foster *(Julianna McCarthy):* the lower class matriarch; mother to Snapper, Greg and Jill; an independent woman with a strong moral code. (She pulled the plug on her dying husband, so expect a lot of suffering for her.)

Greg Foster *(Brian Kerwin):* a lawyer who works with Legal Aid and helps the poor; son to Liz; brother to Snapper and Jill; once in love with Chris, his brother's wife.

Jill Foster *(Brenda Dickson):* a hairdresser; daughter to Liz; sister to Snapper and Greg; momentary wife to the now-deceased Philip Chancellor (the marriage was annulled because his divorce from Kay was not legal); mother to little Philip. A young girl who's had a hard life.

Ron Becker *(Dick DeCoit):* a rapist; husband to Nancy; father to Karen.

Nancy Becker *(Cathy Carricaburu):* wife to Ron; mother to Karen; a sweet, unsuspecting young woman who had a nervous breakdown upon hearing that her husband had raped Peggy.

Karen Becker *(Brandi Tucker):* daughter to Nancy and Ron, about five or six years old; currently living with Snapper and Chris.

REMEMBER ...THEM?

By Peter Z. Grossman

14

Perhaps it will happen at a party or a family get-together. Suddenly there will be organ music or a tune on the radio and one person old enough to remember, will nod and with a knowing smile say, "Our Gal Sunday, the story that asks the question, Can a girl from a mining town in the west find happiness as the wife of a wealthy and titled Englishman?"

Younger people in the room will likely furrow their brows and wonder what that "gibberish" was supposed to mean. But those words were as well known thirty-five years ago, as the cry "Mary Hartman, Mary Hartman!" is today. *Our Gal Sunday,* was a popular radio soap opera. Each day it came on the air to the tune "Red River Valley," and the narrator's voice, reminding the listener of the central question of that rags-to-riches tale.

Our Gal Sunday ran for 22 years beginning in 1937. At that time, radio was regarded as television is now—the principal source of mass media entertainment and information. And even more than today, soaps dominated the daytime air waves. If we can't remember radio dramas ourselves, it's likely that our parents and grandparents can. Many of them were as devoted as any fan of television soaps can claim to be. They tuned in hour after hour, day after day, and knew the Brinthropes, Youngs, and Rutledges as well as current fans know the Hortons, Frames, and Fosters. They could recount a year of plots and probably still can recall high points and choice bits of dialogue. Soap fans are not new. They've been around since the beginning of the genre almost a half century ago.

How did it all begin? Norman Brokenshire claimed that he accidentally discovered the soap audience. In the early 1920s, radio was a new and chaotic medium where almost everything was adlibbed. Brokenshire, an announcer, was waiting for some actors to show up and, to kill time, began reading a short story over the air. He was part of the way into it when the actors arrived and he put the book aside. Over the next couple days, he reported that he received hundreds of letters begging him to finish the story.

Whatever the truth of Brokenshire's claim, soap opera was still several years away. Before it could be successful, three crucial developments had to take place. First, the radio itself had to become familiar. At the time Brokenshire read his story, radio was still a novelty. People who owned a radio would sit around and marvel at any static-filled sounds that came out of it—which was about all that did come out. For theatrical entertainment, people went to the theater or the movie house. In fact, those who lived in rural areas were often so far away from the low power transmitters, that they did not hear radio until the medium was several years old.

A second development was that people had to get used to the idea of a radio serial. They had to begin to listen to one program five days a week and become involved in the story of a set of fictional radio characters. The serial form wasn't new. There were film serials and written serials, in magazines, for example. However a film serial meant that a person would plan to go to the theater for one hour a week (at any one of maybe 20 possible hours). A printed serial could be read at one's leisure. To hear a radio serial, on the other hand, people would have to tune in *every day* at one specific time. Since radios were large heavy objects that had to be plugged into a socket, a listener had to be home (or in some place that had a radio) at the same hour each day.

Finally, before there could be soap opera as we've come to know it, drama had to become a *daytime* radio feature. Traditionally, the day was work time. Those who weren't in the work force—especially housewives—had socializing, shopping, or child care to occupy them. Entertainment was something for the evening and the weekend. Indeed it can be fairly said that all-day entertainment on weekdays went against the work ethic ingrained in American life. The very idea would have scandalized our nation's founders. In order to entice people into listenting to daytime entertainment, radio producers had to find a formula that would first of all, appeal to those most likely to listen—i.e. house-bound women—and that would in time become so familiar that people might be able to go about their chores and still drift in and out of the programs.

While the proliferation of stations and the availability of equipment made the popularity of radio inevitable, there's no doubt that the Depression helped propel it to the forefront of daily life. People simply couldn't afford to go to the theater or the movies very often. It was cheaper and easier to stay home and listen. It was also a ready means of escape from the harsh realities of the world, a more desirable way to pass the time than reading the stock market reports. And it was in the early 1930s that the radio did become the principal medium of entertainment in the country.

Around the same time, America had its first popular radio series. The program was *Amos 'n' Andy*, a nighttime comedy series (not a soap) about two lovable naive black Alabamians who had migrated to Chicago. It was amazingly popular. In 1930-1 it was estimated that over half the people in the country listened to it regularly. Every night of the week for fifteen minutes, life would stop as everyone caught up on the latest doings of Amos Jones, Andrew H. Brown, George "Kingfish" Stevens, and their associates. Not surprisingly, other series like *Myrt and Marge, The Goldbergs, True Romances,* and *Moonshine and Honeysuckle,* quickly followed.

The daylight hours, however, were another matter. Though the nation was growing accustomed to radio entertainment, it still was a nighttime thing. In one representative city, morning brought such off-putting programs as, "Beautiful Thoughts," "Our Daily Food," "Mouth Hygiene," and "The Premium Man." For anyone wanting to be entertained, there wasn't much on the dial to turn to.

But there were already a few who were asking, "If it can work at night, why not in the day as well?" Some experimenting started.

Teacher Irna Phillips, advertising people Frank Hummert and Anne Ashenhurst (later Anne Hummert), and writer Charles Robert Douglas Hardy Andrews (one person), began to explore the possibilities of daytime drama aimed specifically at housewives. All four would become legends of radio soap opera—the Hummerts had more than two dozen shows going at one time by the late 1930s—and Phillips would go on to play a major role in the creation of television soaps. (Though she died in 1973, four of her shows—*The Guiding Light, As the World Turns, Another World,* and *Days of Our Lives* are still on the air.) But Phillips' first effort, *Painted Dreams,* was heard only in Chicago and was not successful. Nor was the Hummerts/Andrews', *The Stolen Husband,* though as the last title suggests, they were on the right track in terms of subject matter.

Clara, Lu, 'n' Em and *Vic and Sade,* neither of which was created by any of the four pioneers, were the first daytime serials to be broadcast on a national network. While they contained some soap opera elements, however, these shows cannot be considered soaps as we know them. *Clara, Lu, 'n' Em* was a semi-improvised rap session between three women who'd sit around talking about themselves and their neighbors. It was more fictionalized gossip than drama. The other show, *Vic and Sade,* was a folksy, humorous serial, a kind of *Amos 'n' Andy,* only with midwestern whites.

Soon after, the Hummerts along with writer Andrews put all the right ingredients together and created a program that was soap through and through. The show, *Betty and Bob,* which premiered October 10, 1932 on NBC, could with a little updating appear on television tomorrow and fans would have no trouble recognizing it. Betty was a secretary who fell in love with and eventually married her boss, Bob Drake, the son of a millionaire. Of course Bob's father objected to Betty because of her humble origins, but that trauma was overcome and the couple embarked on an appropriately stormy married life. The show was successful enough and ran for seven years. Don Ameche, later a movie and television star, played Bob Drake. He was the first of many actors and actresses who went from soap opera to stardom. (Interestingly, *Betty and Bob* was not sponsored by a soap company, but rather by General Mills, the people who make "Wheaties," etc. That fact led one writer to note that if Procter & Gamble and other soap makers had not become so heavily involved in later daytime drama, the genre today might be called "cereal drama" instead of soap opera.)

The success of *Betty and Bob* opened a floodgate. The genre quickly developed a pervasive tone—the one established by *Betty and Bob*—and a format that became *de rigueur* for nearly thirty years. Typically, a soap was fifteen minutes long. It would begin with some theme song usually played with melodramatic portentousness on the organ. Then on came the narrator to announce the program, maybe tell a little bit about it in general, and give a brief update on the status of the story. After twelve minutes of dialogue, the narrator would return with a recap and a question like, "Will Jill marry George? Tune in tomorrow for the next episode of...." Organ music followed—end of show.

There was one other important part of the format that shouldn't

25 of radio's favorite soaps

Just Plain Bill   1933-55

Originally this show was called *Bill the Barber*. It was touted as the story of "a man who might be your next door neighbor," assuming of course that your next door neighbor was the kind of man who could solve everybody's problems.

The Romance of Helen Trent   1933-60

Romance after age 35 for the woman alone. According to the critics, it was a program that gave virtue a bad name.

Ma Perkins   1933-60

Ma and her lumber yard. She even lost a "son" during World War II. As a result she became an effective government spokeswoman.

The Story of Mary Marlin   1935-45, revived 1951-2

What happens when Senator Joe Marlin becomes an amnesia victim? His wife Mary takes over his Senate seat and becomes an advisor to the President while "Never Fail" Hendricks combs the world in search of Joe.

Backstage Wife   1935-59

Mary Noble, wife of matinee idol Larry Noble, faced the problems that are inevitable when 98% of the female population of America is lusting after your husband.

The O'Neills   1935-43

The first daytime ethnic soap. Irish, of course.

The Goldbergs   1936-45

Jewish family in New York and the best known ethnic soap. It ran for six years in the evening, became a Broadway show, and even, briefly, a television series.

Pepper Young's Family   1936-59

Adolescence in soapland. Written by the prolific Elaine Carrington.

David Harum   1936-50

Adapted from a best-selling novel of 1898 and thus one of the more atmospheric soaps. However, it is often remembered more for its promotional stunts than its content. One of those stunts was a contest to rename David's horse. Over 400,000 entries, all of them written on the backs of Bab-O labels, were received.

Big Sister   1936-52

Big Sister was the most popular show on the air for several years. One reason was the love triangle of Ruth Wayne, husband Dr. John Wayne, and Dr. Reed Bannister.

The Guiding Light   1937 (on TV since 1952)-

Irna Phillips' wonder was the first big hit of the bumper soap year in 1937. Need we say more?

Our Gal Sunday   1937-59

Sunday, adopted by two crusty old Colorado miners, grows up and marries Lord Henry Brinthrope.. Can she or can't she find happiness?

Lorenzo Jones 1937-55

> A comical tale of the "lovable, impractical Lorenzo" and his wife, Belle.

The Road of Life 1937-59

> One of the first and the longest running of the medical soaps. ("Dr. Brent, call sur-ger-ee.") It was brought to television in 1954, but didn't stay very long.

Hilltop House 1937-41

> Though not a long-running show, it was notable for one reason: the leading actress was Bess Johnson who played a character named Bess Johnson who later had her own soap called *The Story of Bess Johnson*. Soap opera imitating life imitating soap opera.

Woman in White 1938-48

> Nurses and doctors.

Joyce Jordan, Girl Intern (later, *Joyce Jordan, M.D.*) 1938-48, revived 1951-2

> More nurses and doctors. However it should be noted that from early on, there were women professionals in soap opera.

Young Widder Brown 1938-56

> A woman alone. She ran a tea room and had a thing for wartime medical officers.

Stella Dallas 1938-55

> A superwoman show, billed as "The world famous drama of mother love and sacrifice." (Stop that sheik! He's kidnapped my daughter again!)

Life Can be Beautiful 1938-54

> With Papa David Solomon giving wise advice how could it be otherwise? Nicknamed "Elsie Beebee."

The Right to Happiness 1939-60

> One of the daring soaps in its time. Carolyn had a life more typical of a 70s soap woman than a woman of the 40s. She had three husbands—one of whom she murdered and another of whom she divorced. Also she gave birth in prison. This show was a spin-off from *The Guiding Light*. Yet it lasted over 20 years on its own.

Young Dr. Malone 1939-60

> Further doctors and nurses—especially doctors.

Portia Faces Life 1940-51

> Lawyer Portia Blake defended, prosecuted, and fell in love—not necessarily in that order. Portia came to television in 1954. She left soon after.

The Second Mrs. Burton 1940-60

> Mother versus daughters-in-law. This show was a standard soap for the first twelve years. But in 1952, Hector Chevigny took over the writing in the middle of a case of amnesia and turned the show into a light comedy.

Perry Mason 1943-55

> Perry, Della, Paul, Lieutenant Tragg, etc. A series of mysteries of course. Here was one idea that proved successful on television as well as radio. Not only was the series *Perry Mason* successful; *The Edge of Night* was originally conceived as a Perry Mason type story and it's still going strong.

be overlooked: the commercials. (After all, soap opera got its name from its sponsors.) Usually there were two commercials: one after the opening announcement and the second before the recap. On occasion, however, a commercial was worked right into the scene. (Something like: Kitchen sounds. "Are you busy, Sue? "No, Betty, I'm just cleaning up with this new miracle cleanser called ———" "Oh I use it too. It really makes a kitchen spotless in no time." "Yes, I finished this whole job in ten minutes. Now I'm free to sit and talk with you, Betty." "Oh Sue, it's John...") Compared to today's elaborate pricey commercials, some of the old radio ads seem silly and naive. And surely no sponsor today would allow the line soap-star Mary Jane Higby heard on the air: "And remember, ladies, J.C. Penny is the biggest sheet house in the country." Nevertheless, the shows were effective in pushing products. That fact is apparent when we see that many of the same companies are sponsoring serials 40 years later.

Soap opera was only ten years old when sponsors were clamoring for a piece of the action. Networks began running out of time slots. Soaps went on throughout the day. By radio standards, today's fan is deprived. In the early 1940s, there was at least one, and more often two or three serials on the air for all but one quarter hour between 10a.m. and 6p.m.—over *sixty* soaps every day on the major networks. Seventy-three new programs made their debut between the years 1937-42 alone. And there were actually more than that. Some local stations had their own serials.

Out of the great number of radio serials, over thirty ran for more than ten years. These hits were similar in some respects. They dealt mostly with domestic troubles and were chock full of romance, adventure, and misunderstanding. It's curious that even as writers were spinning out one tale of domestic woe after another, they were evolving the soap opera philosophy that happiness is in the family.

In spite of the similarities of theme and content, soaps came in many packages. Some of those variations might seem hopelessly out of date now, while others will be instantly recognizable to any fan. Still, we can't really appreciate the history of soap opera without a look at the kinds of serials that dominated the daytime radio waves.

ETHNIC SOAPS   Generally, television serials are about the upper middle class and are located in the mythical middle west. The names of characters are pulp fiction American with never an ethnic connotation. *Ryan's Hope* is an exception and some people regard it as a daring experiment. But many radio soaps had prominent ethnic characters, and compared to a program like *The Goldbergs, Ryan's Hope* is a rather light attempt at ethnic soap opera.

The story of Molly and Jake Goldberg, their grown children Rosalie and Sammy, and their neighbors, The Blooms, ran for six years as an evening feature and another nine years during the day. Written by Gertrude Berg, who also played Molly, *The Goldbergs* was about a New York Jewish family. It was ethnic right down to the immigrant accents of Molly and Jake, and the milieu was distinctly New York urban.

The Goldbergs and their neighbors faced domestic crises,

economic troubles, and the unique problems relating to being Jewish in America in the 1930s. The philosophy, however, was vintage soap. The family was triumphant, held in place by the loving mother, Molly. If she was funny at times, it was warm comedy stemming from her inability to grasp the language and the customs of America. (A typical line: "If it's nobody, I'll call back.")

ORDINARY FOLKS   Two of the most popular radio serials were about plain ordinary type people. Instead of the usual upper middle class professionals, *Just Plain Bill* (which ran for 22 years) had as its central character a widower barber, while *Ma Perkins* (27 years) was the story of a widow who ran her late husband's lumber yard. In many respects, the shows were similar. (Some called *Ma Perkins,* "Just Plain Bill In Skirts.") Both had as title characters, down-to-earth folks who had lost their spouses, had grown children, and who spent most of their time being all-knowing and understanding, and helping everyone else out of trouble.

Just Plain Bill, a Hummerts/Andrews collaboration for its first ten years, was about barber Bill Davidson, resident sage of the town of Hartville. Though neighbors and friends often came to Bill for help in solving their problems, he spent much of his time straightening out the lives of his daughter Nancy and her husband Kerry Donovan. Typically, someone would either try to seduce the weak but ultimately faithful Kerry, or Kerry would perceive that sturdy, faithful, occcasionally naive Nancy was about to be led astray. As a result, he'd suffer pangs of doubt/jealousy until Bill would come along to help set his mind in order. The potential seducers—if they actually existed—would either talk to Bill and repent, or they'd be punished appropriately.

Bill was also a guardian of the community and when he was not dealing with domestic problems, he would be called on to face down greedy bankers or conniving gangster types. But no matter who they were, no matter how powerful and ruthless, they were no match for wholesome Bill.

WOMEN ALONE   Perhaps no soap operas played on the fantasies of American housewives like those tales of independent women. Invariably in soapland, such women had rewarding if not glamorous jobs (doctor, lawyer); they met fascinating people; and they were pursued by an army of supposedly handsome, often wealthy, though occasionally corrupt, suitors.

The most successful example of the woman alone was the Hummerts' *The Romance of Helen Trent.* It was on the air for 27 years despite the fact that it was loathed by the critics. It may well have been the most maligned program to survive on either radio or television.

Helen Trent started life on the air as a widow who'd had an unhappy marriage. At the age of 35+ (in 27 years she hardly aged a day), she now faced life alone, working as a dress designer. And of course the men paraded into her life. While she prospered in her work, finally becoming a Hollywood designer, she seemed both hopelessly prudish and incredibly naive. Somehow she managed to fall in love with a steady stream of gangsters, fascists, cut-throats, and would-be rapists. Then again, critics maintained that the latter charge was difficult to substantiate. They claimed that her men got honestly fed up with a woman who once solemnly told a fiancé that being engaged was not a license to hold hands! Year after year, Helen barely escaped one ignoble swain after another. Meanwhile the suffering, good-hearted Gil Whitney stood by, waiting for her to say "yes" to him, occasionally getting shot or beaten by Helen's gangster types while he waited. In the last episode, Helen accepted a proposal from Senate candidate John Cole, perhaps finally to live happily ever after.

SUPER HEROINES A type of daytime drama that has no parallel anymore is the hero/adventure soap. Shows like *Valiant Lady,* and especially *Stella Dallas,* had some of the classic domestic interaction, but they emphasized heroic adventures more typical of Wonder Woman than soap opera. A standard episode of *Stella Dallas* (taken from the Barbara Stanwyck movie of the same name) had Stella commandeering a submarine in order to rescue her ever-kidnapped, married daughter Laurel (Stella called her "Lollie-baby") from the clutches of a lustful shiek. Her other feats during 19 years on the air, included landing a crippled airliner and saving son-in-law Dick Grosvenor from the psychotic millionairess Ada Dexter.

DISEASES AND MEDICS Medical problems are a staple of soap life and have been since the 1930s. From the beginning, writers saw the potential of diseases and other medical problems as a plot device for causing extended periods of havoc and suffering. Though current favorites abortion and alcoholism were taboo on radio, temporary blindness and paralysis of the legs were always going around. And amnesia has been at near-epidemic proportions since the 1940s.

The first case of amnesia was also the longest and, from a plot standpoint, the most important. The program was *The Story of Mary Marlin.* Soon after it reached the air in 1935, Senator Joe Marlin was afflicted with persistent bouts of the soon-to-be-familiar problem. For a dozen years or so, he wandered all over Asia known only as Mr. X. Meanwhile Mary took his place in the Senate—one of the highest ranks a regular soap character ever attained. Curiously, the show lost its audience when Senator Joe reappeared and the dutiful Mary stepped down from her Senate seat in his favor.

Where there are diseases, medical people are sure to appear, and such was the case with soap opera. By 1934, one doctor was featured on *Song of the City* while another wooed poor Peggy Dale on *Peggy's Doctor.* Neither of these shows was successful, but two years later, Dr. John Wayne (not to be confused with the actor) and Dr. Reed Bannister were vying for the affections of the title character of the hugely popular *Big Sister.* After that triumph, many soaps were set around the lives, loves, operations, and illnesses of medical people. Irna Phillips' *The Road to Life,* was the longest running. Drs. Brent, McVicker, and associates lasted for 22 years on NBC.

One of the most popular of the daytime radio healers was *Young Dr. Malone.* For 19 years, Dr. Jerry Malone of Three Oaks experienced the pains and sufferings of the medical side of soapland. In the last episode, for example, Dr. Jerry was getting back his job as head of the clinic and, at the same time, was straightening out the problems between sister Jill and her fiancé's mother. Over the years, Dr. Malone was, among other things, missing and presumed dead during World War II (which provided an opportunity for wife Anne to fall in love with a navy pilot). The good doctor was also sarcastically nominated by James Thurber for a "True Christian Martyr Award" in 1947, when, after he was tried for a murder he didn't commit while at the same time being paralyzed, he suffered an attack of amnesia.

HIGHBROW SOAPS   While *Stella Dallas* might seem a little shallow and cartoon-like, the intellectual and literary levels of daytime radio drama varied enormously. Elaine Carrington's *Pepper Young's Family* was praised by some for its dialogue and characterizations. More impressive still was the short-lived wartime soap, *Sweet River,* by Charles Jackson, who later went on to write the best-selling novel, *The Lost Weekend.*

However, the highbrow king of radio soap opera was Sandra Michael's *Against the Storm. Against the Storm* moved critics to praise seldom given to any daytime drama. "Often sensitive, occasionally poetic," said the usually acerbic Thurber. It went on to win a Peabody Award for distinguished contributions to broadcasting, the only soap so honored.

The program concerned the family and friends of Professor Allen, a teacher at a small college. Though the personal relationships were important, characters also dealt with the issues and ideas of the time. For instance, a significant matter on the show was Dr. Allen's attempt to warn America against the dangers posed by fascism at that time (1939-42). The college setting allowed for leading scholars and writers to appear on the show as themselves. Poets Edgar Lee Masters and John Masefield were among those who performed as guest lecturers of the professor's "class."

INSPIRATIONAL SOAPS   Religion, like medicine, has had an enduring place in daytime drama. Even *The Goldbergs* had Jan Peerce perform the traditional melodies each year on the Jewish High Holy Days. Ministers and priests were characters on other shows. One serial, *Light of the World,* was actually taken from the Bible.

But *the* inspirational soap was Irna Phillips' *The Guiding Light.* The program has been on for nearly forty years without a pause—the daytime drama longevity champion. For a while, it was on both radio and television; in fact, the radio and television versions were identical. *The Guiding Light* went off radio in 1956 after some 19 years, but it keeps going strong on the tube. Since its premiere in 1937, the casts have changed, the characters have changed (Dr. Rutledge, pastor of a Protestant church in Five Points, was the first main character), and even the basic tone of the show has changed. The inspirational messages and sermons have disappeared. Still *The Guiding Light* (now called *Guiding Light*) appears almost indestructible. It usually holds a sixth or seventh place Nielsen rating among daytime serials.

The fact that *Guiding Light* has been able to change over the years, may account for its resilience. No other soap successfully made the transition from radio to television. By 1960, the last radio soaps were gone forever. Dr. Malone, Ma Perkins, Mary Marlin, and the others had departed. There was no place for them in the new medium. Radio couldn't compete with television, and stopped trying.

It wasn't an overnight transition by any means. Television first had to become as integral a part of life as radio had been. Then there was the problem that many women had gotten used to listening to the soaps while they worked in the house. Watching was more engaging. Could a housewife change a child's diapers while her eyes focused on the tube? And there were also problems of cost and logistics. It took time before it was all straightened out.

There was actually a crisis period for television serials in the 1950s. Only CBS consistently upheld the daytime serial . NBC tried and failed over and over again while ABC wasn't trying at all. Even CBS had more washouts than successes. From 1950 when television's inaugural daytime serial, *The First Hundred Years*, bowed until 1960 when radio competition disappeared, forty-one television soaps premiered. Only five—*Search for Tomorrow, Love of Life, The Guiding Light, As the World Turns*, and *The Edge of Night*—survive to this day, and one other—*The Secret Storm*—made it to the 1970s. The losers are now trivia questions: Who remembers serials like *The Egg and I, Hawkins Falls, The Seeking Heart*, and *Date with Life?* And yet they were the inevitable failures along the way—failures that occur in every type of media entertainment.

Soap opera hardly changed during all the years of radio and during the first television decade. Then beginning in the 1960s, the genre suddenly began to change drastically. Even so-called conservative soaps like *Search for Tomorrow*, became less kitcheny, more elaborate, and more reflective of the times. Not so long ago, smoking cigarettes and drinking alcohol were controversial matters. No good characters ever touched anything stronger than coffee. Now alcoholism is a common problem and social drinking is visible daily. There is hardly a subject left that a serial cannot touch, and some soaps try to be as up-to-date and trendy as the latest fashions.

But the changes have only made soap opera more popular than ever, and every sign says that that popularity is growing. We can expect that some of the shows now on television will be there for many more years. Still, today's fans know what it means to lose a favorite show. In the last few years, programs like *The Secret Storm, Love is a Many Splendored Thing,* and *How to Survive a Marriage* were terminated by the networks. But maybe one day, in the not-too-distant future, strains of theme music will bring back cherished memories. Fans will smile knowingly as they recall the Ameses, the Donnellys, and the Kirbys, just as fans of another era remember Helen Trent, Bill Davidson, Stella Dallas, and the other forebears—those long-suffering heroes and heroines, now just the shades of soap opera's past.

Remember them?

CREDITS

References and Credits

(Chapter 1) The letter quoted on page 2 was received by *Daily TV Newsletter,* a publication of Lamplight Enterprises, Inc., New York; the letter quoted on page 3 was originally published in *Soap Opera Digest,* a publication of Soap Opera Digest Publishing Co., New York. (Chapter 2) The letters quoted on pages 5 and 7 were originally published in *Daily TV Serials,* a publication of Lamplight Enterprises, Inc., New York. (Chapter 3) A reference for this chapter was Bruno Bettelheim's *The Uses of Enchantment,* published by Random House, 1976. Dialogue on page 26 is used with the permission of *As the World Turns.* (Chapter 4) The review cited on page 34 was originally published in *Daily TV Serials.* (Chapter 10) The letter quoted on page 111 was originally published in *Soap Opera Digest*; the letter quoted on page 113 was originally published in *Daily TV Serials.* (Chapter 12) Significance of poll results cited in opening paragraph was noted in Martin Mayer's *About Television,* published by Harper and Row, 1968. (Chapter 14) Major sources for this chapter were Raymond William Stedman's *The Serials,* published by the University of Oklahoma Press, 1971; and Mary Higby's *Tune in Tomorrow,* published by Cowel Educational Corporation, 1968.

We thank the publicity departments of the networks for some of the photographs used in this book. Photographs from *All My Children, The Edge of Night, One Life to Live, Ryan's Hope,* and *General Hospital,* courtesy of ABC-TV; photographs from *As the World Turns, Guiding Light, Love of Life, Search for Tomorrow,* and *The Young and the Restless,* courtesy of CBS-TV; photographs from *Another World, Days of Our Lives, The Doctors,* and *Somerset,* courtesy of NBC-TV; photograph from *Pepper Young's Family,* courtesy of the National Broadcasting Company, Inc.

Publisher's Acknowledgments

An entertainment form with so broad a constituency as soap opera must be seen from many perspectives; we have been fortunate to have been able to draw ideas and talent from many sources. Latham would like to acknowledge the substantial contribution of Peter Z. Grossman in those portions of the book which view soap opera within the context of the larger popular culture, and the contributions of Judith Davis in those portions of the book that analyze story content. We should like to thank Carole Deragowski for photographs from the set of *Days of Our Lives*; and Alycia Smith-Butler for photographs from the set of *Love of Life*. Finally, we are grateful for the help and information provided by Pat Palmer, David Houston, and Isobel Silden.

Author's Acknowledgments

James Raftery, press representative for daytime programming (ABC-TV); Wisner Washam, one of the head writers, *All My Children* (ABC-TV); Henry Kaplan, director, *All My Children* (ABC-TV); Bud Kloss, producer, *All My Children* (ABC-TV); John Litvak, former director of *As the World Turns* and currently director of daytime programs, New York (CBS-TV); Joseph Wilmore, producer, *As the World Turns* (CBS-TV); Clarice Blackburn, former associate writer of *Love of Life* and currently actress in *As the World Turns* (CBS-TV); Barbara Duggan, former program coordinator, *The Doctors* (NBC-TV); Kylie Masterson, associate producer, *General Hospital* (ABC-TV); Allen Potter, executive producer, *Guiding Light* (CBS-TV); Leslie Kwartin, producer, *Guiding Light* (CBS-TV); Charles Paul, musical composer and director, *Guiding Light* (CBS-TV); Pamela Paul, music supervisor, *Guiding Light* (CBS-TV); Carlina, music supervisor, *As the World Turns* (CBS-TV); Jean Arley, producer, *Love of Life* (CBS-TV); Thomas deVilliers, associate producer, *Love of Life* (CBS-TV); Aviva Jacobs / Irene Pace, show assistant and production assistant, *Love of Life* (CBS-TV); Claire Labine and Paul Avila Mayer, creators/head writers/executive producers, *Ryan's Hope* (ABC-TV); Robert Costello, producer, *Ryan's Hope* (ABC-TV); Ellen Barrett, associate producer, *Ryan's Hope* (ABC-TV); Mary Ellis Bunim, producer, *Search for Tomorrow* (CBS-TV); Robert Nigro, director, *Search for Tomorrow* (CBS-TV); Charles Dyer, production assistant, *Search for Tomorrow* (CBS-TV); Sid Sirulnick, former producer, *Somerset* (NBC-TV); John Conboy, executive producer, *The Young and the Restless* (CBS-TV); Wendy Dalton, production assistant, *Another World* (NBC-TV); Mary Bonner and Joe Rathenberger, producers, *Another World* (NBC-TV); Lewis Brown, costume designer, *Another World* (NBC-TV); Paul Rauch, executive producer, *Another World* and *Lovers and Friends* (NBC-TV); Otis Riggs, art director, formerly with *Another World* and currently with *Lovers and Friends* (NBC-TV).

And thanks to countless serial performers, whose insights into the serial world helped tremendously, especially Marie Masters (Susan Stewart on *As the World Turns*); John Reilly (ex-Dan Stewart on *As the World Turns*); Kathy Glass (Jenny Siegel on *One Life to Live*); Stefan Schnabel (Steve Jackson on *Guiding Light*); Charita Bauer (Bert Bauer on *Guiding Light*); Ruth Warrick (Phoebe Tyler on *All My Children*); Ron Hale (Roger Coleridge on *Ryan's Hope*); John Gabriel (Seneca Beaulac on *Ryan's Hope*); C. David Colson (Tom Hughes on *As the World Turns*); and John Cunningham (Wade Collins on *Search for Tomorrow*).

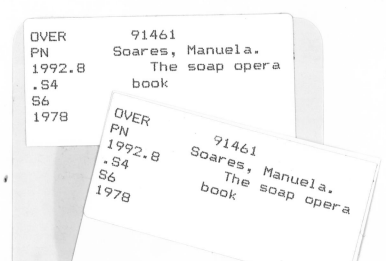